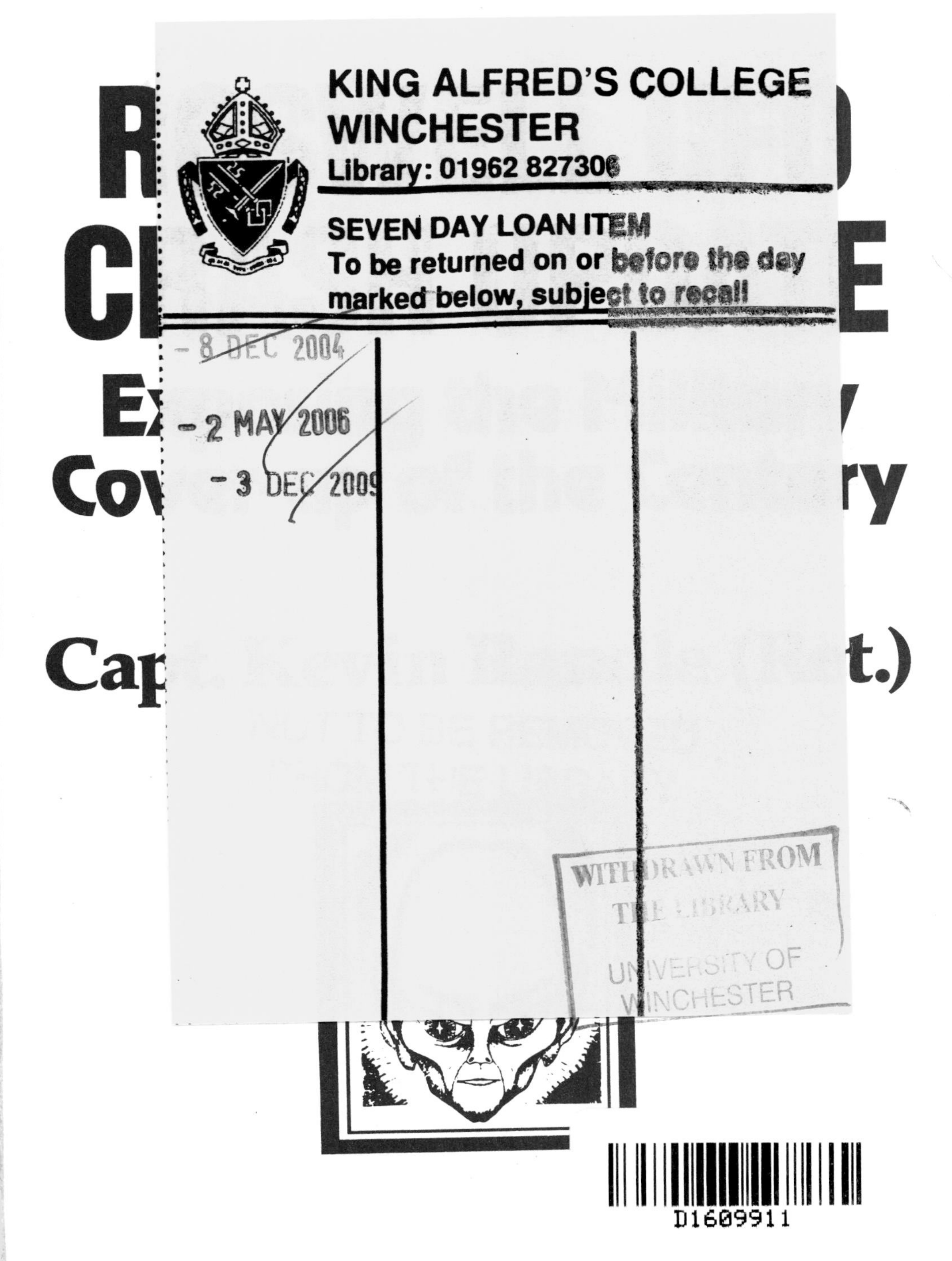

GLOB... ...CATIONS

EDITORIAL DIRECTION
& LAYOUT
TIMOTHY GREEN BECKLEY

ROSWELL UFO CRASH UPDATE

For information: Global Communications
P.O. Box 753, New Brunswick, NJ 08903

Cover art by Barbara Lynn

Composition and design:
Cross-Country Consultants
8858 E. Palm Ridge Drive
Scottsdale, AZ 85260

ISBN: 0-948395-41-5

Contents

Graphics artist Barbara Lynn depicts the scene of the world famous crash of a space craft near Roswell, New Mexico.

Introduction

In the six years that Don Schmitt and I have investigated the crash of a spacecraft near Roswell, New Mexico, a number of very plausible sounding theories have been advanced. Nearly everyone rejects the original solution, a rawin target and weather balloon, provided by Eighth Air Force Headquarters on July 8, 1947. Since that time, others have theorized that the crash near Roswell was a V-2 rocket gone off course, an experimental aircraft such as the Northrop Flying Wing, a Japanese Balloon Bomb, or the atomic weapons housed at the Roswell Army Air Field.

With those theories researched and rejected based on documentation, eyewitness testimony, and contradictions between the facts and the theory, there is little left in the way of a solution. The testimony of many of the witnesses has suggested that what was found were parts of an alien spacecraft. That testimony, from those who were at both identified crash sites seems to eliminate the mundane.

But Karl Pflock, working on a grant from the Fund for UFO Research, has found what he believes to be the solution to part, if not all, of the Roswell mystery. Based on his research, Pflock claims that what was found by Mac Brazel in early July 1947 was not extraterrestrial, but pieces of the highly classified constant level balloon research project known as Mogul. Because of its high classification, and because of the new materials used in the construction of some of the Mogul balloons, Pflock believes that many

The craft impacted the slope slight to the right of the saddle. Army troops surrounded th area to prevent unauthorized visitation.

Photo courtesy Kevin D. Randle

were fooled, thinking they were looking at something that was not made on Earth.

Pflock, in his report for the Fund for UFO Research, *Roswell in Perspective,* examines the whole state of the Roswell investigation as well as presenting the evidence for his theory. To fully respond to that report, it is necessary to counter many of the mistakes made by him. Most are the result of seeing only a portion of the picture. By standing too close, he was unable to see all of it and that contributed to the inaccuracies that crept into his report.

To set the record straight, I have gone into some detail to explain why the testimonies of certain witnesses have been accepted, I provide corroborative evidence to support those conclusions, and present evidence that Pflock has conveniently forgotten. By looking at that forgotten data, the picture is altered, but it does become clearer.

The Air Force entered the debate recently with their own report on what crashed on the Brazel ranch. They agree with Pflock, believing the debris was caused by the remains of a Mogul balloon. Pflock thought it was Flight No. 9 made on July 3. The Air Force disagrees with that, believing instead, that it was Flight No. 4 made on June 4. There are specific problems with both these theories and those problems will be examined at length later.

This wasn't the first explanation that Pflock had offered concerning the Roswell case. After Pflock's first visit to Roswell, I began to hear that he believed he'd solved the mystery. Jack Rodden, a professional photographer living in Roswell reported he'd met with Pflock, but instead of an interview, Pflock spent the time suggesting the crash was nothing more extraordinary than a Northrop N-9M Flying Wing.

Rodden wasn't the only one to be treated to Pflock's first solution. In a telephone call with both Dr. Mark Rodeghier and Don Schmitt, Pflock again suggested the wreckage was from a flying wing. Again he suggested the N-9M wooden mock-up. According to both, Pflock was convinced that he had solved the Roswell case.

It took twenty minutes in the library to put the theory to rest. The last flight of the N-9M was May, 1946. The aircraft, a two-engine flying mock-up of the larger XB-35, was made of steel tubes, plywood, and various conventional components. Nothing used in the construction was extraordinary or could be easily misidentified.

But, to be thorough, I checked the flight records of the XB-35, the full-sized flying wing, learning that in July, 1947 all had been grounded. Lieutenant Robert Jones, public information officer at Muroc Army Air Field told reporters at the *Chicago Daily News* that, "None of our flying wings has been in the air recently." They had been grounded in November, 1946 because of gear box problems. Besides, according to all available records, none of the XB-35s crashed.

The jet powered version, the YB-49, did have a fatal crash. Captain Glen Edwards was killed during a test flight and Muroc was renamed in his honor. That crash, however, took place in California in 1948. The first flight of the YB-49 was in October 1947, so none of them could account for the Roswell crash.

With the documentation eliminating the first theory, Pflock reinvented the balloon. It wasn't a rawin target device as suggested by the Army, but, as Pflock would have us believe, a balloon belonging to Project Mogul. It is clear from the available testimony of those involved and from the documentation, that balloons were being launched in the right time frame in the right locations in New Mexico. By ignoring a large body of eyewitness testimony, by accepting as accurate the statements of three civilians who were only marginally involved, Mogul could be suggested as a viable explanation.

For the reader—those on the outside who have neither the time nor the money to make an exhaustive investigation of the Roswell case—it is necessary to supply all the data. Too often these reports and investigations are treated as debates with one side looking to defeat the other. That might make interesting entertainment, but it does nothing to advance our understanding of the situation. The only way for the reader to understand what happened at Roswell is provide as much data as possible. That is the real purpose for this report. Unfortunately for the reader, to make a point crystal clear, it is sometimes necessary to repeat information already reported.

So rather than limit the scope to argue against either Pflock's Mogul theory or the Air Force Mogul theory, I have expanded it to include necessary information about many of the witnesses. I have tried to explain, as fully as possible, why certain conclusions were drawn. Naturally, my own bias will be evident to the reader. I believe what crashed at Roswell was an alien spacecraft, *but* that belief is the result of six years of investigation.

With no apologizes for the tone, I present the other side of the case. It is now up to the reader to look at all the evidence and decide what he or she wants to believe. I think that all intelligent people will agree with me. The evidence seems clear cut and obvious. However, I have learned that many can look at the facts and arrive at different conclusions. That doesn't make them bad, stupid, or liars, it just means they have a different opinion, and I would hope that we could dispassionately discuss those differences.

Regardless of that, here are the facts as I have been able to determine them. They are based on the work of a great many people. Without Don Schmitt, the work would never have been done. Tom Carey was invaluable. Dr. Mark Rodeghier, often seen as a neutral, has provided a great deal of assistance.

It is now up to the readers to decide what is correct and what is not. I believe, however, when all the evidence is examined, the conclusions will be obvious...Mac Brazel found the metallic remains of an alien spacecraft.

First Lieutenant Walter Haut, under orders from the 509th Commanding Officer, issued the press release that claimed the Army had recovered a flying saucer on a ranch in the Roswell region.

Photo courtesy Kevin D. Randle

Part I: The Case for a Crash at Roswell

Captain Sheridan Cavitt at first claimed that he hadn't even been in Roswell when the crash took place. Later he confirmed that he had been to the crash site with Lewis Rickett and possibly Jesse Marcel, but said he saw only the remains of a balloon.

Photo courtesy Kevin D. Randle

The Truth About the UFO Crash at Roswell

It is true that Don Schmitt and I place enormous confidence in the eyewitness testimonies of Jim Ragsdale and Frank Kaufmann. It is also true that if their testimonies were stand alone, meaning there was no independent corroboration for them, the case would be significantly weakened. However, it must be remembered that both men claim first-hand knowledge, that their observations are corroborated by many others, and they are is two more first-hand witnesses than had been interviewed prior to the publication of *The Truth About the UFO Crash at Roswell.*

But the testimony offered by them is not stand alone. Many aspects of their reports have been corroborated by others who were clearly in Roswell in July 1947, and who can prove it. It is because of that documentation and corroboration by those others, that the testimonies of both Ragsdale and Kaufmann take on added significance.

The Date of the Crash

For years it has been claimed that the crash took place on the evening of July 2, 1947. Almost everyone who wrote anything about the crash used the July 2 date. In my first book, *UFO Crash at Roswell,* I used the same date. There was no reason to dispute it then.

The question, however, is where did that date originate. On July 8 the *Roswell Daily Record* reported that Dan Wilmot saw an object 15 to 20 feet in diameter over Roswell and heading to the northwest on the previous Wednesday, July 2. Although there was no reason to make the assumption, there were those who believed that this is the object that crashed. In fact, Charles Berlitz and William Moore in *The Roswell Incident* make the claim that the object Wilmot saw on July 2 was the one that crashed on the Brazel (Foster) ranch. All dates flowed from there until Walter Haut, the public relations officer of the 509th Bomb Group, reported the "Roswell Army Air Field" captured a flying saucer on July 8.

"The Fizzle in the Sky"

The skeptical community has complained frequently that no one saw the craft in the sky. Suddenly, Mac Brazel appears on the scene with a field filled with strange metallic debris. Major Jesse A. Marcel, air intelligence officer of the 509th reported that "It was something that must have exploded above the ground and fell..." But the point is that neither man saw anything in the air.

That changed with the appearance of William Woody. Woody, later interviewed by Clifford Stone, Dr. Mark Rodeghier, Schmitt and me, said that he and his father were working outside in the cool of the late evening and were surprised when the wall of the house lit up. Turning, they saw a bright light moving quickly through the sky on a downward arc. He said the light was so bright that they couldn't look directly at it, comparing it to the flame of a welding torch.

Following the conventional but inaccurate wisdom, this means the Woody sighting took place on Wednesday, July 2. Woody said that he and his father drove out, a day or two later, to search for the object. They drove north of

Roswell, along Highway 285, but weren't allowed to turn off the main highway onto any of the dirt roads because military officials were there to stop them. Woody believed they made the trip on the weekend, but couldn't be sure.

However, if we continue to follow the conventional wisdom, which is the military didn't enter the case until the following Tuesday, July 8, it means the Woodys waited nearly a week before beginning their search for the downed object. Woody's testimony didn't fit, exactly, into the scenarios developed from the conventional wisdom. It was one of those little problems that nagged at the back of the mind because it didn't fit into the framework of the case properly.

The date of the conventional wisdom changed with the appearance of a written record. In Roswell, at the Saint Mary's Hospital, Franciscan Catholic nuns Mother Superior Mary Bernadette and Sister Capistrano were making routine observations of the night sky. They saw the bright object plunging toward the ground late on the evening of Friday, July 4. There has been a suggestion they saw nothing more mysterious that a Fourth of July fireworks display, but that explanation is weak. The nuns had seen fireworks earlier. This was nothing like those.

Jim Ragsdale was only a mile or so from the impact site. He witnessed the object roar over head, slamming into the ground. Like Woody, he described the brightness of the object as similar to that of a welder's torch. The next morning he was apparently on the site when the military caravan arrived. From a distance, he watched as they cordoned the immediate impact area, the MPs taking the high ground.

Witnesses at two other locations also watched the object in the night sky. Archaeologists saw the object as it fell. Corporal E.L. Pyles was stationed at a small facility away from the main Roswell base. He saw the bright object as he crossed the parade ground on the main base and believed that it was late at night, and thought it might be close to the weekend. He said that he thought, at first, it was a shooting star, only bigger. As it crossed the sky, it seemed to get larger and there was an orangish glow or halo around it. A few days later, when he heard the balloon explanation offered in the *Roswell Daily Record,* he didn't believe it. What this does is establish his sighting in the proper time frame prior to the press release on July 8, 1947 even though from memory he could only place the event in 1947.

We now have a better picture of when the crash took place. We now have solid evidence for July 4 rather than wild speculation for July 2. It makes the Woody story fit the scenario. Rather than waiting several days, Woody and his father go in search of the object on the weekend. The military cordon, according to Ragsdale, and 509th Provost Marshal Edwin Easley, was already erected.

And, there is one new piece of evidence. In July 1947 Leo B. Spear was an MP with the 1395th MP Company in Roswell. Although he didn't see anything himself, he did say that he remembered other MPs returning from the crash site talking about the flying saucer. Spear said that he believed the story to be "BS" until he read about it in the paper a day or two later. What this does is confirm, from still another source, that the military was involved prior to July 8. It corroborates aspects of the story told by Ragsdale, Kaufmann, Pyles, Woody and the Catholic nuns.

Although these observations have been written off as an astronomical phenomenon by some, there is no evidence to support that conclusion. Rather, we have observations that do have enough in common to allow us connect them. We have an bright, white object low in the sky (below 20,000 ft.) that fell to earth late at night in early July, 1947, about 11:30 PM on Friday night, and based on the data available it seems to be the object that was recovered outside of Roswell.

The Shape of the Craft

The conventional wisdom has always been that the object was a domed disc, the classic flying saucer. Gerald Anderson, whose testimony has been thoroughly discredited, talked of a domed disc. Other sources, primarily second hand, suggested that it had been a disc-shaped object.

Kaufmann was the first to suggest the object was not disc shaped but was, in reality, heel shaped. Although the idea hadn't been suggested in relation to the Roswell case prior to his testimony, it wasn't completely without precedence. Kenneth Arnold didn't see a flying saucer, but something that was heel shaped. In the official Project Blue Book files, the illustration Arnold drew is definitely heel shaped.

Project Blue Book files contain another heel-shaped object, this one photographed on July 7, 1947 as it flew over Phoenix, Arizona. Project Blue Book officers labeled the case as a hoax, but not for very good reasons. If the object at Roswell was heel shaped, then the reason for the Air Force opinion is obvious. This in no way "proves" that a heel-shaped object was found near Roswell, but it does confirm that such objects were being seen and reported.

One other man, Lewis Rickett, a counterintelligence agent at Roswell in 1947, said that the object had been heel-shaped. Those were his words, spoken to Don Schmitt just days before Rickett died.

The Location of the Crash

The corroboration extends beyond the timing and shape of the craft. Both Ragsdale and Kaufmann speak of a crash site north of Roswell, about 35 miles from the base.

Ragsdale mentioned using the Pine Lodge Road to get there. Kaufmann said the military used Highway 285 and then drove cross county. The military officials later realized Pine Lodge Road was the best way to get to the impact site.

The location of the crash, north of town, has also been mentioned by Rickett, Dr. W. Curry Holden and Major Edwin Easley. Holden was north of Roswell, not far west from Highway 285. Easley provided notes indicating that the crash site was north of Roswell, but not far northwest, near Corona.

There is still another first-hand source who wishes to remain anonymous who has also corroborated the exact site as given by Kaufmann. He used the book, *Roads of New Mexico* to pinpoint it for me since it was impossible to take him out there given his location. Granted, such testimony does nothing for those who aren't privy to it, but it added another corroboration for the crash site location for me. He had no knowledge of what either Ragsdale or Kaufmann had told me.

Dr. C. Bertrand Schultz said that while traveling north out of Roswell on Highway 285 he saw the military cordon. The soldiers were stationed to the west of the highway but since Schultz had no desire to drive in that direction, he didn't care. Later, after Holden told him what he had seen, Schultz realized the importance of his observations.

It should also be noted that the location of the impact site, about eight miles from the main highway, made it difficult for the soldiers to set up the cordon out of sight of the highway. To do so would have required them to erect their roadblocks almost in sight of the impact site. It made more sense for the soldiers to block the roads near the highway and not allow anyone to divert from it than it did for them to try to hide their presence.

The location close to Roswell was also corroborated by Dr. George Agogino (second hand), who corroborated the testimony of the "anonymous archaeologist" who had spoken to me on the telephone. The archaeologist said that he had been working the area north of the Capitan Mountains in central New Mexico. That fits with what has been reported by others. Agogino told Tom Carey (a researcher living in Pennsylvania), after Carey had read my notes of the conversation with the anonymous archaeologist to him, "That's what he told me." The archaeologist has been identified and his story has been corroborated by named sources.

Frankie Rowe's (second hand) father, Dan Dwyer, gave her general information about the location. He suggested that it was north of Roswell, but closer to the city than the conventional wisdom suggested. Barbara Dugger (third hand), whose grandfather was Sheriff George Wilcox, agreed with that. It was her impression that the crash site was in Chaves County, near Roswell, not in Lincoln County near Corona.

Two Locations

Everyone agrees that there was a debris field found by Mac Brazel, and nearly everyone agrees that there was a second site, where the craft and bodies were found. Originally it was suggested that this second site was far to the west, on the Plains of San Agustin, but no first-hand testimony has developed to corroborate that theory. Now, based on the eyewitnesses, it seems clear that the second site was close to Roswell. And now there are those who corroborate two very distinct sites.

Brigadier General Arthur Exon, one time commander of Wright-Patterson Air Force Base, reported that he had flown over both sites. He was clear on that point. There had been two distinct sites. He mentioned tire tracks on them and reported the gouge that corroborated the tale told by Bill Brazel.

Brazel, who saw the site days after his father's discovery, told Don Schmitt and me about the gouge through the center of the debris field. According to him, the gouge was about 500 feet long and about ten feet at the widest. He mentioned that it had taken two years for it to completely grass over.

Robin Adair, a technician for the Associated Press in July 1947, said that he had been required by the AP to rent an airplane in El Paso, Texas to fly to Roswell. He'd flown over two sites, and saw soldiers at both of them. In fact, Adair said that the soldiers had tried to wave him off as the plane circled the area, flying low. Neither site was near the Plains, but both were north and northwest of Roswell.

Frank Kaufmann and a Few Mistakes

The skeptics, not happy with the testimony of first-hand witnesses, present a case for rejecting the testimony given by Frank Kaufmann. They seem to believe that rejecting Kaufmann will weaken our case. While that is not true, Kaufmann is an important source of data. Karl Pflock suggests Kaufmann is not to be believed. For example, Pflock, in his lengthy report, writes, "As we approached the end of our conversation, Kaufmann mentioned having a copy of an issue of the *Congressional Record* in which his name appeared...Although I said I was very interested in seeing the *Record,* he never offered to show it to me." Pflock suggests that Kaufmann was vague about it, "Humming and hawing around." (I might point out that, according to Pflock himself, he made no recording of this conversation. Instead we're treated to Pflock's perception of what took place, including the remarks inside quotation marks and attributed to Kaufmann. And, I might also note that Kaufmann disagrees with Pflock's analysis of the situation.)

The truth is, the 91st Congress, 2d Session, Senate Document No. 91-71, entitled *Congressional Recognition of Goddard Rocket and Space Museum, Roswell, New Mexico with Tributes to Dr. Robert H. Goddard,* was published on May 28, 1970 by the US Printing Office. While not the Congressional Record by precise standards, it certainly is a Senate Document. Kaufmann's name, but the way, appears on page 37.

Kaufmann, in fact, called this a Congressional Recognition, and it seems that Pflock is the one who misinterpreted Kaufmann's statements as meaning it was the *Congressional Record.* And, it is a Congressional document. Even if Pflock had been right about Kaufmann calling it part of the Congressional Record, isn't Pflock's criticism splitting hairs and therefore irrelevant? The document does exist but Pflock didn't take the time to get all the facts before writing off this portion of Kaufmann's story in his attempt to discredit Kaufmann's testimony.

Pflock makes much of Kaufmann's alleged claim that Charles Lindbergh had been in Roswell. Pflock, during an interview with Kaufmann, wanted to know if Lindbergh had been part of the recovery team. Pflock writes, "Later in the conversation I attempted to learn more about the 'others.' Because of the testimony of another witness at that time known only to me, I asked Kaufmann if he had ever heard anything about Charles Lindbergh being involved. After a long pause, he replied, 'Yeah, yeah. He was one of the group. He was there.'"

In all the interviews that Don Schmitt and I conducted with Kaufmann he had never hinted that Lindbergh was "one of the group." Lindbergh was not associated with the recovery of the object but it is clear that he had been to Roswell. Earl Zimmerman reports that he had seen Lindbergh at the Roswell Officer's Club, in the company of Brigadier General Roger Ramey, commander of the 8th Air Force. Many history books report that Lindbergh consulted with the officers of the Eighth Air about the use of atomic weapons during this period. And, of course, the Senate Document provided by Kaufmann also establishes Lindbergh's presence in Roswell during the dedication of the Goddard Museum, corroborating another aspect of Kaufmann's testimony.

But the main point that is overlooked in Pflock's criticism of Kaufmann is all the corroborative testimony. It wasn't just his testimony that lead to the various conclusions about the date of the crash, the shape of the craft or the location of the impact site, but that provided by a number of other witnesses. Edwin Easley, for example, corroborated the location just north of Roswell. As did first-hand witnesses Jim Ragsdale, W. Curry Holden, C. Bertrand Schultz, and William Woody.

An archaeologist, whom Pflock labeled as "Indiana Jones" in a subtle attempt to belittle the testimony, revealed a great deal of information that turned out to be accurate. He said that he had been working north of the Capitan Mountains which I took to mean in Lincoln County, but with the impact site now located, he could easily have meant an area to the northeast of the Capitan Mountains. His story, matches that provided by other witnesses, and reinforces what Kaufmann has said. And Dr. George Agogino who heard the story from the same source and has corroborated the testimony.

In fact, much of what Kaufmann said has now been reinforced by others who had no way of knowing what Kaufmann had reported. As we have seen, Lewis Rickett used the same words in describing the shape of the craft, calling it heel-shaped. His description of the impact site location, close to Roswell, and his description of the strange metallic debris matches that provided by Kaufmann.

What we have, then, is a number of others, from Edwin Easley and Lewis Rickett to W. Curry Holden, who have added to our knowledge of what happened in July 1947. They have corroborated what Kaufmann said, a fact that seems to be lost on Pflock and other critics. They always mention Kaufmann, forgetting that there are many others now reporting the same facts.

The final criticism is Kaufmann's use of various pseudonyms. It is important to remember that Kaufmann is not responsible for the various names used to identify him. Most of those were invented by me to protect his identity. Joseph Osborn was created because I wanted to assign a name to him for the ease in writing about his testimony without revealing who he was. The Osborn name was not supposed to see the light of day. That was a mistake I made in trying to complete material for a deadline. I had meant to remove it and insert a note that the witness wished to remain, for the moment, anonymous.

Mr. X was invented by Stanton Friedman in violation of an agreement. When we met in Chicago to discuss the validity of Gerald Anderson and the theory of a similar crash on the Plains of San Agustin, I refused to tell Friedman who our source was. Because it was unfair to use testimony from a source I refused to reveal, I agreed not to use any of the testimony, believing that my case against an event on the Plains was strong enough without it. Friedman violated that agreement by trying to refute the testimony and labeling Kaufmann as "Mr. X."

Speculation about the Barney Barnett case arose, not from Kaufmann, but from his suggestion that a number of "fake" sites had been created to divert attention. Don Schmitt and I assumed that one of those was Barnett because the Barnett testimony, as it stands, does not fit into the framework at all. Besides, there was the diary kept by Ruth Barnett that tends to eliminate Barnett as a witness to any event involving a crashed saucer, a fact that Pflock and other critics seem to have overlooked. Kaufmann told us to ignore the Barnett case and it appears that his advice was good.

There is one other fact that is relevant. Kaufmann has been interviewed by a number of high-powered Washington, D.C. attorneys, former high-ranking military officers, and one prominent journalist. Each of these people have been impressed with the credibility of Kaufmann. At this point, there is no reason to reject the Kaufmann testimony, especially when it is remembered that is corroborated by many others who were also involved.

Jim Ragsdale and a Few Mistakes

Pflock, in his report, also takes the testimony of Ragsdale to task, suggesting there are some things that are not verifiable. Unfortunately this gives the impression that the Ragsdale testimony can't be believed, but when the facts are examined, the conclusions change.

Pflock writes, "...Ragsdale was familiar with the impact site area, where he claimed to have been camping with his lady friend, because he was working nearby as a member of a survey team blazing the route for a new El Paso Natural Gas Company pipeline...Two long-time residents told me they remembered the pipeline being built sometime in the 1950s, not the mid-1940s. If their recollections were correct, this would raise a serious question about Ragsdale's credibility."

If the situation was as Pflock described it, then the Ragsdale's credibility would suffer. However, that is not the case. In the initial interview with Ragsdale, he mentioned the pipeline as a landmark today. He used it to try to orient the location on the maps used. In the January/February issue of the *IUR* Schmitt and I write, "Ragsdale was familiar with the area, being employed to survey natural gas lines through the region to the north." We were trying to explain, but failed, that he had been into the area frequently *after* the event because of his work. We did not mean to imply that his familiarity came because of survey work in 1947. In fact, Ragsdale said nothing at anytime that would lead to that conclusion. If others have drawn it, it is because of poor communication on our part rather than anything said be Ragsdale.

Pflock goes farther, explaining that when he first called the Ragsdales, Mrs. Ragsdale told him he had the wrong man because "Jim didn't move to Roswell until 1959." The truth is, Mrs. Ragsdale did not want to talk to the man (Pflock) and told him that Jim hadn't moved to Roswell until 1952. Ragsdale, however, in 1947, lived in Carlsbad, not that far south of Roswell.

Mrs. Ragsdale also reports that on two separate occasions, they received telephone calls from men who claimed to be from Washington, D.C. and suggesting that if they didn't consent to an interview, they would be subpoenaed. The Ragsdales didn't respond to the treats.

The Changing of the Ragsdale Tale

Ragsdale has told his story for many years according to others who have been interviewed. Other members of the family have heard it and believe it. Other researchers, including Dr. Rodeghier heard Ragsdale's son confirm the report, proving, if nothing else, that the family was aware of the tale for a long time.

But there are some emerging problems with the Ragsdale story. For example, Ragsdale now claims that he did not stay away from the crashed craft as he originally said, but worked his way down close to it, attempting to pull the helmet off one of the dead aliens. The eyes, according to Ragsdale's new testimony, were large black ovals. What he is offering is a description of the grays. The eyes, according to other witnesses were not large and oval, but shaped like human eyes, just slightly larger than normal. In our original interviews he said that he hadn't gotten close enough to see any facial features.

The question is, do we reject Ragsdale now, or can we believe some of what he says? Of course I have an affidavit from him, a tape recording of what he said during the first interview with Don Schmitt, and the notes I took during the second and third meetings. And, now there is the statement that he made in September 1994 which is in conflict with those earlier interviews. What is the motivation for that new statement? What does it tell us?

First, it seems that someone who is familiar with the UFO field has been talking to him. It is not someone who is especially well versed, but someone who might have read a couple of books about UFOs and knows a little about the abductions. The size and shape of the eyes of the dead creatures is the clue. The grays, which have been portrayed on the covers of many UFO books, have provided the new evidence for Ragsdale.

Second, there has been a major change in Ragsdale's personal life. When Don and I first spoke to him, he had an interesting story told by a first-hand source. Now, with his financial situation changed, he has desire for money. To tell of being close enough to try to remove the helmet made a better tale than one of seeing something he thought of as a dummy in the distance. The financial situation is important enough for him to begin to take cues from those in a position to offer money as an inducement.

There is no question about the financial arrangements. I have seen a document that is an agreement with Ragsdale offering him money for his story, to be handled "exclusively." Now that money has changed hands as a partial payment for his story, Ragsdale's credibility as a source has been seriously compromised.

It is also clear that he was picking up cues from those offering the money. What isn't known is if he discussed the story with those offering the money, trying to find ways to improve it, or if the coaching was subtle and unconscious. Whatever the method, it is clear that he has been coached. It is clear that he has changed the story so that it fits in with the conventional wisdom but not the Roswell facts, and was changed because of the perceived financial opportunities.

Personally, I believe his original story. I accept it because of the way he was discovered and because his story was corroborated by others. Don and I have, since this new story surfaced, again spoken to family members, and have learned that he had told, basically, the same story for years. The changes have perplexed them as well. They don't understand why the story has been altered.

We must be willing to admit that these latest revelations have seriously damaged the credibility of Ragsdale. If it was not for the original interviews, if it was not for the corroboration provided by other sources, the Ragsdale testimony would have to be discarded. Fortunately we have enough data about his original statements that we can make some judgments about the case. Because of that, we know that his testimony isn't completely worthless. We know that there is a core of solid data.

Unfortunately, as a witness with future potential, Ragsdale has been eliminated. Clearly anything he says to us in the future must be examined very carefully in the context of what has happened in the past. His reputation has been seriously damaged by his attempts to make money on his first-hand observations just north of Roswell.

So, we find ourselves in a dilemma. Ragsdale has altered his testimony. Do we reject all of it? Some of it? Part of it? None of it? And how do we decide?

For me, I have looked at all the data. I have discussed the data with Ragsdale, his family and his friends. I have seen the areas of corroboration. I accept the original testimony because of that. I accept it because of how it fits into the Roswell case. And, I reject the new data because it is so clearly the result of coaching that took place in the last few months. And even with that I am still bothered by Ragsdale.

An investigation like this is an evolving and changing beast. There are those who have their own reasons for talking or investigating. All that must be taken into consideration. Ragsdale has altered the scenario he offered but the conclusion remains the same. We eliminate, from the equation the data that does not fit because of the investigation, and look at what is left. In the end, we have Jim Ragsdale on the scene of a crash of an alien spaceship. Everything else is so much smoke designed to obscure the truth and I wonder if that might be the real motive.

The Archaeologists

It has been suggested by critics that the claim the archaeologists have been found is premature. The question is, how can it be premature when the leader of the expedition said that he had been there. Dr. William Curry Holden said that the location was north of town and responded that the military had been there. In response to direct, careful questioning, Holden repeated that he had been on the site. What he said also corroborated the stories reported by Ragsdale, Kaufmann and others.

Holden, according to the biography contained in the Southwest Collections at Texas Tech, was born in Coolege, Texas on July 19, 1896. He attended the Rotan High School and then taught for a year or two at a rural school in Fisher County, Texas. He entered the service in 1918, but a year or so later, after separation from the military, was the principal of the Rotan High School for the 1919–1920 session.

In 1920 he enrolled in the University of Texas and graduated in June, 1923. He was an instructor at a junior college in Abilene, Texas but continued his education, receiving his M.A. in 1924, and eventually received his doctorate in history.

Holden ran much of his archaeological site studies on a shoestring and conducted his first field work in 1929 in the panhandle area of Texas. In 1930 Holden excavated a site near Pecos, New Mexico. His field trips alternated between sites in central Mexico and the Arrowhead Ruin near Pecos. He was also involved in excavation of caves in western Texas and worked other sites in east-central New Mexico.

Interestingly, his work in archaeology, as well as his ethnographic and ethnohistorical research, provided him with information to write both non-fiction works and novels. His *Hill of the Rooster* (1956) was called by Yaqui Indian leaders as one of the best portrayals of the Yaqui. In contrast, he published a number of non-fiction works detailing the history of West Texas.

Holden was married twice and had one daughter, Jane Holden, whom he described as "the professional" meaning that she was the anthropologist and archaeologist while he was a historian.

Holden ended his long and distinguished career as the chairman of the department at Texas Tech and as Professor Emeritus of History. In July 1947 he taught a summer session at Texas Tech. It was a graduate seminar.

Holden was 96 years old when we learned that he had been involved in the events of July 1947. Because of his age, I made arrangements to interview him as quickly as possible. On November 21, 1992, I visited Holden in Lubbock, Texas.

Although Holden was elderly when I visited him, he seemed to be in good health, living at home. He was a tall, thin man who looked to be frail, but who still moved easily. Because of the circumstances, I had only thirty minutes or so to speak with him. Given those circumstances, and Holden's relative good health, I planned to speak with him again. This was just a preliminary interview conducted to verify his participation in the events near Roswell in 1947. Unfortunately it was not recorded. I fully expected to meet with him again to record his testimony and clarify the situation.

In the course of an investigation, it is best not to provide any information to the subject of an interview prior to that interview. That prevents contamination and means that the information retrieved is pure. With Holden it was necessary only to mention that I was interested in an event outside Roswell in 1947 and let Holden fill in the details about the crash and the retrieval.

Holden said, "I was there. I saw it all, but it was so long ago."

That was, of course, exactly what I wanted to hear. It meant that Holden was one of the long, lost archaeologists. And it looked as if he had been the leader of the expedition. Here was a man who had been on the impact site just north of Roswell where the craft and bodies were found.

But that wouldn't be the last of it. First, it could be argued that he hadn't understood the question. Second, it could be argued that he had, in fact, understood the question, but had answered it the way I wanted it answered. Finally, it could be argued that he hadn't heard the question, hadn't bothered with an answer, but because of his age, was just talking to fill the silence.

A 96 year old man can't be questioned in the same way that one half his age can be. Over the last few years, given the length of time between the event and the interviews, I have gained some experience in questioning the elderly. In the first few minutes it becomes clear how reliable the testimony is. "Fleck" Danley, Barnett's boss in 1947, was elderly when I spoke to him in October 1990. I knew after speaking to him briefly that Danley was easily confused and no longer had a clear recollection of the Barnett's telling him about the crashed saucer. To continue the interview would have been useless and would have contributed nothing more than confusing detail to an already confused case.

Holden, on the other hand, seemed to have a firm grasp on the reality of the situation. While it would have been a simple task to lead him, that was not the point. I needed to gain information that would help us understand the Roswell case. I wanted to give him no clues as to my mission and by doing that, I could be certain that his answers were as honest as he could make them.

It is probably necessary to point out that some critics have suggested that Holden was too old to provide valuable information. However, many of those accept the testimony of the elderly if it happens to parallel their own thinking. *The Skeptical Inquirer* (Summer 1994) reports that one of the most famous Loch Ness Monster photos had been faked. According to the article, the stepson (Christian Spurling) of one of the men involved, confirmed the photo was bogus. According to the article, "Although 90 and in poor health, he [Spurling] was able to answer a series of questions."

The point here is not to argue about the validity of the belief in the Loch Ness Monster, but to show that CSICOP (Committee for the Scientific Investigation of Claims of the Paranormal) does accept the testimony of the elderly. Because a witness is old, it does not mean his testimony must be rejected out of hand. And, just because

Holden was 96, it doesn't mean that his testimony is flawed. It must be taken as part of the whole so that we can understand what happened.

Holden confirmed that the crash site had been just north of Roswell, off the main highway leading out of town, but he had no recollection of the exact location. He wouldn't have been able to find it on a map, other than provide a very general location west of the highway and north of the town.

Holden didn't provide a good description of the craft, suggesting only that it wasn't a flying saucer in the classical sense of the word. It was more rounded toward the front, with a scallop at the rear. He never got too close to it, seeing it from fifty or sixty yards. He, and those with him, had thought it was some kind of government experiment and didn't want to intrude. Later, during their interrogation at the RAAF, they learned that the government had nothing to do with it, and that it was, in fact, something made on another world.

According to the story, as confirmed by Holden, one of his students had gone in search of a telephone to report the find to the local authorities. The military responded, though Holden didn't remember if any civilian authorities, police or fire, had. The archaeologists were rounded up by the military officials, warned that what they had seen was a matter of natural security, and escorted from the site.

Although Holden said nothing specific about it, and I didn't ask about it, it seems the archaeologists were taken back to the base at Roswell for a complete debriefing. Because Holden was back in Lubbock on July 9 to make a bank deposit, according to the available records at Texas Tech, it seems that this aspect of the case lasted only a few hours, certainly no more than a day.

Holden confirmed that there had been bodies, but

again, he was vague about it. He thought they were smaller than humans but he remembered very little about them.

Again, I supplied no hints as to what I wanted from him. I tried to ask the questions in a very non-direct way, waiting for him to introduce a concept before exploring it. Holden, for example, mentioned those killed in the crash and I merely asked if he remembered what they looked like. When he said something about a crumpled craft, I asked what it looked like.

But I had to be careful with the questions because I didn't what it to sound like an interrogation. And, I didn't want him to anticipate me. I asked him three different times if he had been there, even phrasing one of the questions negatively, in case he was picking up verbal clues. Holden told me each time, "I was there."

What Holden had done, under the careful and admittedly gentle questioning, was corroborate the information we had received from other sources including Frank Kaufmann. Holden understood that we were talking about the crash of a ship outside of Roswell and I wondered, in his long association with the field of anthropology and archaeology if he could help identify the people who had been there with him. His response was only, "I was there."

Before I left, I asked if it would be all right to contact him again, either on the telephone or if I made it back to Lubbock. Both he, and his wife, said that it would be fine, though he had trouble on the telephone because of poor hearing. Mrs. Holden, however, mentioned to me quietly that her husband, though in good health, was elderly and was easily confused. His mind was no longer as sharp as it had once been. She had never heard the flying saucer story from him and thought that he was mistaken.

This was the second Mrs. Holden though she was his wife in 1947. According to her, she accompanied him on all the expeditions, did the record keeping and the cooking. He did make some short trips which she didn't. These were day long, or two day long affairs exploring west Texas and southeastern New Mexico. She also said that she didn't believe that he had been involved in the Roswell events, his statements to the contrary.

Holden's daughter, Dr. Jane Kelly, echoed the claim. She said that he had never mentioned a thing about the crash or the bodies to her. She was sure he would have, had it actually happened. She also said that he sometimes jumbled his memories, coming up with a new sequence that he was positive was right, even when documentation from others showed he was mistaken.

All of Holden's records were donated to the Southwestern Collections, which is part of the library on the Texas Tech campus. It seemed like an easy task to check his research diaries for the appropriate dates and find out exactly where he was on the critical weekend in 1947.

Holden, however, didn't keep chronological diaries. Instead, he keep diaries on specific topics. In other words, to search for the important information, we had to know what he had been working on and then search that specific diary. The task, in that direction, seemed nearly impossible.

However, we advised the people there that we were interested in Dr. Holden in early July 1947. Anything they could provide us would be helpful. They mentioned his banking records, his income tax returns, and various boxes of university and related correspondence were available. Clues might be obtained in those records.

According to the documents, Holden wrote a check to the Lubbock Rotary Club on July 3. He made a bank deposit on July 9. Both these documents suggest that he was in Lubbock on those two days.

In addition, Holden was invited to a wedding on the

evening of July 8. There is nothing in the record to show whether or not he attended that wedding.

The *Bulletin of the Texas Technological College* (now Texas Tech University), *Division of Graduate Studies* reveals that during the summer session, 1947, he taught a seminar for three semester hours. The catalog shows that it was a seminar in history.

The catalog also reveals that Holden taught classes in Field and Museum Technique and in Southwestern Archaeology in the Anthropology division of the Department of History and Anthropology during the spring session 1947. In other words, there is nothing conclusive in the catalog especially when it is remembered the events in Roswell took place over a three-day weekend and that Roswell is less than two hundred miles from Lubbock.

Nothing in the records revealed where Holden was on the critical weekend. He could easily have made the trip to Roswell with a few of his students for any of a number of reasons. There were a number of archaeological sites in eastern New Mexico that Holden had been to on several occasions. He could have been in New Mexico or he could have been in Lubbock.

We are not left, however, with no way to corroborate Holden's story. He did speak to colleagues about the events. Dr. Charles Bertrand Schultz, a vertebrate paleontologist from the University of Nebraska, had originally provided the clue that lead us to Holden.

According to Schultz, interviewed a number of times by Tom Carey and me, including one video taped session in May 1993, he'd heard the story from those involved shortly after it happened. Schultz was in Roswell, according to him, on the critical weekend, but saw nothing of the crashed ship or the bodies. However, when leaving Roswell, and driving north along Highway 285, Schultz said that he had seen the military men who were part of the cordon. They were all to the west of the highway, and since Schultz had no desire to drive in that direction, it didn't bother him.

Later, from Holden, he heard the rest of the story, including information about the crash, the craft, and the bodies. Schultz, in the years that followed, shared the story with family members, including daughters Donna Wilcox and Tranda Schultz. Both have said their father told them of the flying saucer crash while they were growing up.

Records at the University of Nebraska, including the field research notes, fail to establish where Schultz was on the July 4, 1947 weekend. Later in the week, Schultz was at an early man site called Lime Creek in southwestern Nebraska. He worked the site with Dr. W. D. Frankforter.

Frankforter, according to Carey, has corroborated Schultz's report of the crashed saucer. He too, heard it long ago and was aware of Holden's involvement.

When I visited with the Holdens, both said they remembered Schultz. Mrs. Holden said that he had visited them several times in Lubbock. And, documentation from the Holden collection at Texas Tech confirms they were together in December 1947. At the forty-sixth annual meeting of the American Anthropological Association held at the University of New Mexico, Albuquerque, Schultz presented a paper on the Lime Creek site. Although Holden didn't present a paper there, he was one of those who attended the conference.

There is one other aspect to this. In the course of the investigation, I have run into a couple of former military officers who suggest they have been involved in the Roswell case. They seem to be in possession of knowledge that far outstrips those with just passing interest in the case. I have been able to corroborate much of what they had told me in the past. When I have questions, I sometimes ask them, and receive guidance from them. However, since they refuse to go on the record, I use them as one more level of corroboration, but if they are the only source of information, I don't use it. Without being able to provide others with names and sources, information developed about Roswell from them is next to useless. Independent researchers must be able to corroborate the work or there is no reason for anyone to accept it as accurate.

Given that qualification, I can say that these men have also confirmed Holden's involvement in the Roswell case. They have said that he was the leader of the archaeological expedition. If it wasn't for Holden's own confirmation, plus that of Schultz, it would seem that the question was open for debate. However, there is enough corroborative testimony to allow the conclusion to be drawn that Holden was there, as he claimed, and that he did see it all, just as he said.

Holden, however, gave us the answers to some of the questions. Even though I had only the single opportunity to interview him and we didn't go into detail, he did answer a few of my questions.

Although I had planned to interview Dr. Holden again, to formulate a list of questions and carefully ask them, all on audio tape, that didn't happen. Dr. W. Curry Holden passed away not long after I spoke to him in Lubbock. He died on April 21, 1993.

New First-Hand Corroboration

Don Ecker of *UFO* and John Price of Roswell's UFO Enigma Museum (6108 South Main, Roswell, NM 88201) discovered another first-hand witness to the craft and the bodies found outside of Roswell in July 1947. Thomas Gonzales was a sergeant assigned to Squadron T of the 509th, and, according to him, helped in the guarding of the craft and the bodies. Don Ecker writes in the UFO,

"When asked what the main body of the craft looked like, he described it more as an 'airfoil' than the more commonly known disc, and described the bodies of the 'little men' not as 'greys' but as more human-looking beings."

Ecker also interviewed other members of the family and learned that they had known about the Roswell story for years. He had told them that Gonzales had once had a piece of debris from the crashed spaceship. Gonzales' son confirmed that there had been a strange piece of metal that was "odd" and that couldn't be marked or scratched. Unfortunately, like so many leads toward a piece of the debris, this one has not yet borne fruit.

What is most important here is a new witness, found not by Don Schmitt or me, but located by other researchers. The initial interviews by Ecker and Price were conducted before we learned of the existence of the man and those interviews were video taped. It can't be claimed that we had "lead" the witness, or that we had contaminated him before he was properly interviewed. But most importantly, he corroborates much of what has been said by Frank Kaufmann, Jim Ragsdale, W. Curry Holden and Edwin Easley. He corroborates the location north of town, the craft being "an airfoil" as opposed to a domed disc, and that the bodies were of "little men" and not the grays reported in the abduction research.

Conclusions

The point of all this, is to demonstrate that there were a number of interviews conducted, that the majority of them are on either audio or video tape (audio tapes at CUFOS, video tapes at FUFOR), and some of the interviews were witnessed by others. Many of the witnesses, such as Frank Kaufmann, have been interviewed by many people. Family members, friends, and former military companions verify parts of the stories. There is a wide variety of corroborations for these tales.

If we eliminated the Ragsdale and the Kaufmann testimonies, would we be left with a gap in our knowledge about the location of the impact site? No. It would be a little more difficult to put the whole picture together, but it could be done. For example, we could pinpoint the location based on the interviews conducted with Easley, Holden, John McBoyle, Woody and Schultz (talking about a military cordon off Highway 285), and Exon and Adair.

If we eliminated the Ragsdale and the Kaufmann testimonies, could we determine the shape of the craft? Again, the answer is yes. Rickett provided us with a very good description, as did McBoyle, Easley, and the archaeologist to whom I spoke on the telephone. And now Thomas Gonzales tells of the airfoil that he saw.

Could we describe the recovery without Ragsdale or Kaufmann? Again, yes. Easley provided some detail, as did Rickett, McBoyle, Holden and the archaeologist. Second-hand sources, Rowe and Dugger also provide data.

Flights out of Roswell containing material or bodies have been described by various crew members including Marcel, Robert Porter, Robert Slusher, and Len Stringfield's pseudonymous "Tim." Others, such as Robert Smith, described loading various aircraft with crates that held debris.

Second-hand sources, Sappho Henderson who said her husband flew wreckage to Wright Field, and John G. Tiffany who said his father was on an aircraft that might have held bodies, also describe flights.

There has been a large number of reports about bodies, from Edwin Easley's first-hand comment about "Oh, the creatures," to Thomas Gonzales description of "little men," to the second hand testimony of Glenn Dennis about the look of the alien creatures including a drawing based on what he was told. Ruben Anaya also told a second-hand story of alien bodies. As did Melvin Brown who claimed to have seen the bodies.

What this demonstrates is there is a large body of corroboration for the testimony of both Ragsdale and Kaufmann. There are important, additional first-hand sources who saw a great deal and have reported it. There are second-hand sources who add detail to our knowledge. If we listen to what they say, we can reconstruct the events of July 1947 without Ragsdale or Kaufmann.

This shows that Ragsdale and Kaufmann are not alone in what they saw or they reported. Their stories have been verified and corroborated. And if they were alone in what they said, they tend to corroborate one another, and that is the point overlooked by too many.

The question that must be asked is why is this testimony being rejected when single eyewitness reports have been accepted in the past. Why is this testimony being rejected in favor of second-hand reports? Why is it being attacked when there is so much supporting evidence for it? Why is that supporting testimony ignored? Is there another agenda at operation here? And if so, why?

It has been suggested that Roswell investigators should be more cautious after the Gerald Anderson episode. That suggestion is correct. We were very cautious before we accepted the testimonies of Ragsdale and Kaufmann. We waited for verification and corroboration, which we found. For those who don't believe, they should initiate their own search. What they will find is that Ragsdale and Kaufmann are telling the truth.

Jesse Marcel, Jr. and his mother, Viaud, outside their house in Helena, Montana.

Photo courtesy Kevin D. Randle

The Report on the Conclusions of the Recent Air Force Analysis of the Roswell Incident

Ever since Don Schmitt and I began our reinvestigation of the Roswell case, there have been those throwing explanations at us. Many of them were serious attempts to explain the facts. We expect that from those in the UFO community. We were surprised when the Air Force joined the chorus. They had been silent on the topic of the Roswell crash for more than forty years. Suddenly they had reinvestigated the Roswell case and they had an answer for it.

According to the news release, dated September 8, 1994, the Air Force investigators claimed to have reexamined all the files and documents related to the events outside of Roswell in July 1947. Their conclusion was that the debris recovered was not an alien spacecraft as others believed. Like Karl Pflock, they believed it was nothing more extraordinary than a balloon from the top secret Project Mogul.

Air Force investigators, reviewing the records, inter-

Frankie Rowe said that her father, a Roswell fire fighter, made a fire run to the site north of Roswell. Later, she had an opportunity to handle a small piece of debris and was threatened by a man in an Army uniform.

Photo courtesy Kevin D. Randle

viewing five witnesses, and studying the various documents and books about Roswell, determined that the debris found by Brazel was from Mogul launch No. 4 on June 4, 1947. This, according to the records, was made of a cluster of standard meteorological balloons, a sonobuoy (microphone) and nothing else. In other words, it was just a weather balloon as the Army Air Forces said. The Air Force had identified the specific project implying there was something special about the balloons used. The records showed the balloons were ordinary.

Like Pflock's *Roswell in Perspective,* the Air Force report seems to make a very solid case for the belief. It is not, however, the conclusions of an investigation as they suggest, but the result of an orchestrated debate. The Air Force, as the prosecution, has presented their side of the controversy. Naturally, wanting to convince us of the validity of their conclusions, they have given us nothing from the other side. They have structured the report so that it is a persuasive argument proving that the debris came from the top secret Project Mogul and was, in reality, the remains of a balloon. But now it's my turn.

Ranch manager Mac Brazel has been described by friends and family as an old time cowboy. He lived south of Corona, New Mexico in a house that had neither running water nor electricity. The area was so isolated that his closest neighbors were ten miles away. The family, according to Bill Brazel, son of Mac, spent most their time in Tularosa, New Mexico so that the kids could go to school. One neighbor said that they were all happier that way.

Mac, according to the legend, heard a strange explosion one night while a thunderstorm raged. The next morning as he was checking the pastures to see where the rain had fallen he came across a field filled with metallic debris. Tommy Tyree, a ranch hand hired after the event, remembered Brazel telling him that the debris field was so densely packed that the sheep refused to cross it. Had it been a small area, Brazel probably would have cleaned it up and said nothing to anybody. Major Jesse Marcel, Sr. said the debris was three-quarters of a mile long and two to three hundred feet wide.

Brazel collected some samples of the material and showed them to his closest neighbors, Floyd and Loretta Proctor. Floyd, though interviewed by others, has since died. Loretta has been interviewed a number of times and has said that she "didn't know what the material was." Floyd tried to whittle on it with his pocket knife but couldn't make a mark. Brazel held a match up to it to show that it wouldn't burn.

On Sunday, July 6, Brazel drove into Roswell. Bessie Brazel Schreiber claims that she accompanied her father on the trip. While he was at the sheriff's office, she, and her younger brother were elsewhere in town. That, of course, explains why there was never any mention of her presence at the sheriff's office.

After showing some of the strange material to the sheriff, who in turn called the intelligence officer at the Roswell Army Air Field, Brazel was interviewed by the sheriff. Brazel then lead Marcel, and Captain Sheridan Cavitt, to the debris field. By the time they reached the area, it was too late to accomplish anything. That night they stayed at the Hines House. Marcel checked a chunk of the debris with a geiger counter but found no signs of radiation.

The next morning Brazel arrived with two horses. Marcel, interviewed by Bob Pratt, said that he couldn't ride but that Cavitt, a good west Texas boy could. Marcel said he would follow in the jeep carryall.

Marcel and Cavitt spent the day on the debris field. In the Pratt interview, Marcel said, "Well, we found some metal, small bits of metal, but mostly we found some material that's hard to describe. I'd never seen anything like that...[O]ne thing I do remember...I wanted to see some of this stuff burn...I lit the cigarette lighter to some of this stuff, and it didn't burn." He also described "little members, small members, solid members that you could not bend or break but it didn't look like metal. It looked more like wood." Marcel said they were weightless. "You couldn't tell you had it in your hands. Just like you had balsa wood."

During the interview Marcel said something that turns out to be extremely important. He said, "It was something that must have exploded above the ground and fell. And I learned later that, farther west, towards Carrizozo, *they found something like that, too.* That I don't know anything about. [It was] the same period of time, sixty to eighty miles west of there."

What Marcel has done here is speak about the second site. When interviewed so many years later, he had the directions wrong, but he had no doubt there was a second site. And, if there was, then the idea of a Mogul Balloon, as proposed by the Air Force, has been seriously damaged.

About dusk, Marcel sent Cavitt back into Roswell. Marcel wanted to stay a little longer, continuing to search the area. This means, according to Marcel, he and Cavitt had spent all day trying to clean an area where a Mogul balloon had come down. When he left, there was still debris scattered on the field.

Although Marcel and Cavitt had left Brazel alone that day, he was not through with his involvement. On the evening of July 7, radio station owner Walt Whitmore, Sr. drove to the ranch and picked up Brazel. They returned to town, Whitmore inviting Brazel to stay with him. During the late evening, Whitmore interviewed Brazel using a wire recorder. He planned to broadcast that interview the next day, July 8.

The broadcast is never made. George "Jud" Roberts, the minority owner reported that phone calls from Washington, D.C. ordered them not to broadcast the interview under any circumstances. Roberts was told if they did broadcast the interview, they would have twenty-four hours to find new employment because they would no longer be in the radio business.

Brazel had stayed with Whitmore and there is some discussion that Whitmore, on the morning of July 8, drove Brazel out to the base. Although this is unconfirmed, it is clear that Brazel next surfaced in the custody of the military. They escorted him to the offices of the Roswell Daily Record. Paul McEvoy, Floyd Proctor, and Lyman Strickland all said that Brazel had been brought to the office by military officers. Proctor even reported that Brazel went out of his way to avoid speaking to his friends. Unfortunately all three men are dead.

There are, however, others still living who saw Brazel in the company of the military. Leonard Porter and Bill Jenkins saw Brazel escorted through Roswell by military officers. Frank Joyce said that there were officers with him when he stopped by the offices of KGFL on the evening of July 9.

Brazel wasn't allowed to leave Roswell once he had been reinterviewed. According to his son, Bill, he read a story about his father in the Albuquerque newspaper and knew that his father would need help on the ranch. He drove down on Saturday, July 13 or Sunday, July 14. When he arrived, there was no one there. His father returned two or three days later.

Major Edwin Easley knew that Brazel had been held at the base. He said that Brazel stayed at the guest house guarded by the military police.

Marian Strickland said that she remembered Mac Brazel sitting at her kitchen table drinking coffee and complaining about being held in jail. While being held at the guest house isn't jail, he wasn't allowed to leave so it amounts to nearly the same thing.

The questions that arise from this testimony, much of it on video or audio tape, are interesting. If what Brazel found was nothing more than a weather balloon, even one launched by those working on the highly classified Project Mogul, why the effort to hide the truth? Brazel is dragged under military escort to the various media outlets in Roswell to tell his balloon story. Why did they care at all? After all, it is nothing more, according to the Air Force, than a balloon. Wouldn't the flying saucer story offer the perfect cover for Project Mogul? Why not just let that story run because it would take interested parties in the wrong direction? They would be looking for something up near Corona, and not at Alamogordo, where Mogul was temporarily house.

Of course there is another question that begs an answer. If the balloon explanation is the correct one, why was Brazel held by the military for more than a week? Testimony from his son, as well as the neighbors, supports the story of Brazel in military custody for several days.

The Air Force in their report does not deal with any of this evidence or these questions. Instead, they reprint part of an article published on July 9, 1947 in the *Roswell Daily Record*. They use it to establish a time frame for a Mogul launch but are unimpressed with Brazel's statement, "I have found weather observation balloons on two other occasions. This was nothing like them."

But like all those who report on this newspaper story, the Air Force leaves out the last paragraph. It says, "I (Brazel) am sure what I found was not any weather observation balloon...but if I find anything else, besides a bomb they are going to have a hard time getting me to say anything about it."

That last statement becomes very important when the records of Project Mogul are reviewed. Especially when it is remembered that Launch No. 4 was nothing more than a cluster of weather observation balloons and rawin targets. Of course, we must assume that the rawin targets were attached because this flight was designed, according to Dr. Charles Moore, to train the Watson Lab personnel track the balloons. There is, however, no documentation to corroborate that assumption.

The Second Site

Although Marcel opened the door to the second site in his many recorded interviews, the Air Force didn't bother to enter. Instead, they ignored all testimony that would lead in that direction, pretending that it didn't exist. If the stories of a second site were nothing more than the second-hand ramblings of family members, then the testimony might be considered very weak and unimportant. However, there is a body of additional testimony to lead in that direction. Testimony from those who were on the second site and can speak of it and the craft and bodies in the first person.

These witnesses have located that site just north of Roswell, about thirty-five miles from what had been the front gate of the base. Some of the references are vague while others are very precise. All lead to the conclusion there was a second site where the craft and bodies were located. If true, this testimony calls the Project Mogul explanation into serious question. If there were two sites, then the Mogul explanation simply doesn't work. And, if there was a site where a craft and bodies were found, no conventional explanation can explain the facts.

Many people spoke of a site just north of Roswell, not far to the northwest near Corona. William Woody reported to seeing something bright in the sky west of

Roswell. It seemed to be dropping toward the ground. It can be argued that what Woody reported was the craft just prior to the crash. If that is the case, the question that comes to mind is what would have been burning on the cluster of balloons. They were, after all, filled with helium, an inert gas.

Woody's testimony, however, is more important because of another aspect. He, along with his father, drove north out of Roswell during the July 4 weekend, either on Saturday or Sunday. To the west, on the side roads from Highway 285, they saw soldiers blocking the way. When they tried to turn in that direction, they weren't allowed to leave the main highway. There was no reason to block those roads for the recovery of a Project Mogul balloon. In fact, there is no evidence that any roads were ever blocked when any Mogul equipment was being recovered.

The testimony of a man who was a boy in 1947 might not be considered as the most reliable. Dr. C. Bertrand Schultz, a vertebrate paleontologist working near Roswell, was heading north on Highway 285 that same weekend. According to him, he saw the soldiers standing along the dirt roads to the west. He didn't want to drive in that direction so wasn't that interested in them.

Later, he learned from a colleague, Dr. W. Curry Holden, that something had crashed. Holden, interviewed just before his death in 1993 said that he had been at the site north of town where the craft and bodies had been found. To Schultz, it was clear that the military men he saw were part of the cordon of the area.

Jim Ragsdale, a civilian, in talking about the location of the crash site was asked by Don Schmitt, "How far from town?" Ragsdale said, "Thirty or forty miles."

Army counter-intelligence agent, MSGT Lewis Rickett also suggested a site close to Roswell. In a taped interview with Don Schmitt, he said, "I remember it took us about

45 minutes. I said, 'How far are we going out here and he (Sheridan Cavitt) said, 'It's just over here..."

Major Edwin Easley, who had been responsible for cordoning the area said that the site was closer to Roswell, north of town. He made no mention of a location far to the northwest, near Corona, probably because the Debris Field was of little importance when compared to the Impact Site were a craft and bodies were located.

There are some second-hand witnesses who reported what fathers or grandfathers had said. Frankie Rowe, whose father was a fire fighter with the Roswell department, said that he made a run outside the city limits to where the bodies had been found. She believed that it was close to town. And, there is no evidence that the Roswell Fire Department ever made a run into Lincoln County to the site of the Debris Field.

Barbara Dugger said that her grandmother, Inez Wilcox, told her that her grandfather, Sheriff George Wilcox had been to a site no more than thirty miles from Roswell where the craft and bodies had been discovered. Although Mac Brazel did visit the Chavez County sheriff, rather than the Lincoln County sheriff, there is no evidence that Wilcox, or his deputies made a trip outside of the county. Family members said that he and his deputies had been turned back by the military cordon.

All of this suggests a second site closer to Roswell. There is testimony of two distinct sites. Air Force investigators apparently stayed away from any testimony that would lead to the second site. They spoke to no one who would suggest there might have been another site, including Air Force Brigadier General Arthur Exon.

During a taped interview in May, 1990, Exon said, "It was probably part of the same accident, but there were two distinct sites. One, assuming that the thing, as I understand it, as I remember flying the area later, that the damage to the vehicle seemed to be coming from the southeast to the northwest, but it could have been going in the opposite direction, but it doesn't seem likely. So the farther northwest pieces found on the [Brazel] ranch, those pieces were mostly metal."

Exon was saying, based on his first-hand observations, that there were two sites and that the farther to the northwest site was mostly metal. In other words, Exon's observations corroborated the information that there was a second site, that the Brazel ranch contained mostly metal, and that there was another site closer to Roswell.

Although it is clear that the Air Force investigators had access to all these data, that they had read both the books, they didn't bother to interview General Exon. If they had asked, I could have played the tapes for them.

The Unusual Metallic Debris

It is interesting that in the Air Force report mentions only those who handled debris that could have been seen as something from a Project Mogul balloon. Although there are dozens who handled various types of metal, the Air Force ignored them. Again, it is clear that they wanted no testimony that would suggest there was something truly unusual about the debris.

The military was the first to offer an explanation in 1947. Within hours of First Lieutenant Walter Haut's press release, the Army Air Forces was saying that it was nothing more spectacular than a balloon and radar reflector from a rawin target balloon. Brigadier General Roger M. Ramey, at Eighth Air Force headquarters in Fort Worth was telling all who would listen that the officers at Roswell, caught up in the excitement of the flying disc craze had misidentified the balloon.

This ignores, of course, the fact that the men at Roswell were hand picked because of their expertise. All were highly trained individuals selected because of their professionalism. After all, this was the only nuclear strike force in the world at the time. The second string was not involved at Roswell.

For the moment, however, ignore that. Suppose that Major Jesse A. Marcel, Sr. was fooled by the foil, balsa and string of the normal rawin balloon (such as those that were part of the Mogul array train) and believed that he'd located something extremely unusual. His first action was, of course, to transfer the debris from the crash site northwest of Roswell to the base there for examination.

According to Marcel's records, and the testimony of his son, Marcel had been trained in radar operations. Assuming that his training did not include any information about the balloons, it seems reasonable that Marcel would have been aware of them. According to the 509th Bomb Group unit history for 1947, Marcel's staff included a radar interpretation officer. Again, that training might not have included work with balloons, especially those designed to assist the weather officer in the gathering of weather data or those used in a top secret project.

Marcel, however, as the air intelligence officer for the group, would have been privy to the data collected by the weather officer, and to the types of equipment, including balloons used to gather it. In other words, there was nothing secret about the gathering of weather data that would have prohibited Marcel from seeing the operation or examining the equipment used to gather it.

And while it can be argued that Marcel had no need to know about the top secret Project Mogul, again, the equipment was not secret. Even when they began using the polyethylene balloons in July, the balloons were not classified. It is almost impossible to believe that Marcel, when he examined the debris the first time, would have been lead to comment on the extreme unusual properties of it had it been nothing more than a rawin target balloon. And even if not cleared to know of Mogul (which he was not) the balloons, according to the Air Force, were, in fact, weather balloons. Nothing extraordinary about them.

Two facts impact on this. First, the rawin target balloon (which was part of the Mogul array train), according to various meteorological sources, was first used in the late 1920s. It was originally designed with a highly reflective appendage that allowed those on the ground to visually track it as it climbed through the atmosphere. Later it was adapted to use with radar sets. Irving Newton, a weather officer at Fort Worth in 1947, said that he'd launched hundreds of such balloons during the invasion of Okinawa at the conclusion of the Second World War. The rawin target balloon was not of a new or unusual design that could have fooled all the highly trained men at the 509th Bomb Group.

Second, on or about July 1, Sherman Campbell, a farmer living near Circleville, Ohio spotted the remains of one of the rawin target balloons on his ranch. Campbell, who was not trained in intelligence work, realized that he had found a balloon but believe it might explain some of the flying disc reports because of the shiny reflector carried aloft by the balloon.

Campbell called the local sheriff, who identified the balloon as mundane immediately. The local newspaper was also alerted and an article about the find was carried by the press. The story, including a picture of Jean Campbell, the daughter (misidentified in the pictures as Campbell's wife) appeared in newspapers around the country.

No one in Ohio thought the balloon was anything but a balloon. The military didn't investigate, didn't fly the debris to another part of the country, and didn't issue a press release about the find. Everyone involved, with no training at all, recognized the balloon for what it was. This in contrast to the mistakes made by trained personnel in New Mexico.

The Roswell Cover-up

Overlooking all that, meaning the possibility that a mistake had been made, there is the testimony of Colonel Thomas J. DuBose. In July, 1947 he was the chief of staff of the Eighth Air Force and knew exactly what was going on. He said, repeatedly, on both audio and video tape, "Actually, it was a cover story, the balloon part of it...I don't know whether it was McMullen (Major General Clements McMullen, Deputy Commander of the Strategic Air Command) or Kalberer (Colonel Alfred Kalberer Eighth Air Force chief of intelligence) or who, somebody cooked up the idea as a cover story...we'll use this weather balloon. That was the direction we were told. I mean, there wasn't any question about it. We were told this is the story that is to be given to the press and that is it and anything else, forget it."

According to Colonel DuBose, there was no question that the cover story had been designed to get the reporters off General Ramey's back. Give them an explanation that they'll accept but don't tell them the truth.

With all that testimony, from the participants, and from the facts, it would seem that the balloon explanation would fade from the scene. Clearly something crashed at Roswell and just as clearly it was not a balloon. Balloons were used as a cover to eliminate speculation about the identification of the object that crashed.

It must be remembered that, according to the Air Force report, they believe that the debris was the result of a Project Mogul balloon. What the Air Force doesn't bother to mention is that Launch No. Four, the culprit according to them, was made up of normal meteorological balloons and the possibility that rawin targets were attached. In other words, they offered a new solution that was the same as the old. A weather balloon with a rawin target.

Other types of balloons, experimental aircraft, rockets and missiles, and secret projects of all sorts have been suggested as alternative explanations of the crash at Roswell. Ignoring, for the moment, the fact that no one has been able to produce any documentation that conclusively proves this, an examination of all the testimony will eliminate all these explanations. To make any one of them work, it is necessary to reject the eyewitness testimony from multiple sources. When all the facts are examined, such alternatives slid beneath the waves.

Any of the alternatives might be acceptable if there were no witnesses to the crash. Prior to this, the conventional wisdom had always been that no one saw the object in the air before the crash. The debris had been found, already on the ground, by rancher Mac Brazel. Searches initiated after the fact located the remainder of the craft and the bodies, according to this scenario.

But sources at three separate locations witnessed the crash. Jim Ragsdale, a long time New Mexico resident saw it come down in flames, during a lightning storm about 11:30 P.M. on the evening of July 4, 1947. A balloon wouldn't have come down in flames and wouldn't have been visible at night.

And remember that William Woody described the object, as it fell out of the sky, as resembling a meteor. A bright white meteor trailing red. He watched it long enough to get a very good look at it. Since Woody was east of Roswell, and the debris field that Brazel found, and the impact site where the craft was recovered, are both far to the north of Roswell, the balloon explanation is again eliminated.

The observations of both these witnesses also eliminates the experimental aircraft. What sort of experimental aircraft was being tested in New Mexico...at night...during a storm? Again, there are no records available any where that attest to any type of balloon experiment or experimental aircraft test late on the evening of July 4 that could account for the debris. The Air Force has concluded the same thing after searching their records.

And, remember, all this was observed by another party. The Catholic nuns provided documentation about the crash occurring on the evening of July 4. This date alone suggests that it had nothing to do with any experiments, clandestine or other because everyone had the day off.

The other aspect that must be considered is the testimony of Frank Kaufmann, assigned to the base at Roswell. The object, whatever it was, had been watched on radar as it flew over southern New Mexico, off and on, for nearly four days. If it had been anything belonging to the United States, if it had been a research balloon, experimental aircraft, or a rocket from White Sands, the men at Roswell, or their superiors such as Brigadier General Martin F. Scanlon had the authority to discover it. Had such been the case, their observations would have been suspended under orders to protect the secrecy of the project, but they were not.

When the first-hand testimony covered only the debris field and the wreckage recovered there, speculation about its nature could be made. That is, until all the eyewitness testimony was reviewed carefully.

Marcel said about the debris, "I'd never seen anything like that. I didn't know what we were picking up." He said that some of the debris was a thin as newsprint, feather light but so strong they couldn't dent it or burn it. He described foil-like material, I-beams, and "...other stuff there that looked very much like parchment that didn't burn."

Marcel was so impressed by what he had seen that he stopped at his house on the way back to the base. He wanted his wife and son to see the debris. When Jesse Marcel, Jr. saw the strange material, he asked his father what it was. Marcel, Sr. "It's a flying saucer."

Marcel, Jr. said that he saw some foil material that was thicker than lead foil and that was much stronger. He mentioned the I-beams which seemed to be made out of layered foil and that was embossed with writing. Marcel, Jr. described the writing as, "Purple. Strange. Never saw anything like it.

Within a couple of days, Marcel, Sr. returned to the house and told his family that they were not to mention what they had seen. It was now highly classified and they weren't to tell anyone about it. Of course no one would have cared had they only seen the remains of a Project Mogul balloon because the fact balloons were being used was unimportant. In fact, it was so unimportant that the newspapers carried stories about the cluster balloons being launched from Alamogordo and that could explain some of the flying saucer sightings. In those newspaper reports they even provided enough data that Soviet spies, had they been inclined, could have discovered what Mogul was.

Mac Brazel, who found the debris field, was not interviewed in person, having died more than two decades before the case developed, but his son, Bill Brazel was. In the months after the crash, Bill Brazel, while riding that portion of the range searched for pieces of the metallic debris. He found a few, according to him, "...oh not over a dozen and I'd say eight. There were three items involved. Something on the order of balsa wood and something on the order of heavy gauge monofilament fishing line and a little piece of... it wasn't really aluminum foil and it wasn't lead foil."

Brazel said the wood-like piece would flex a little. "I couldn't break it and I couldn't whittle it with my pocketknife...The only reason I noticed the tin foil was that I picked this stuff up and put it in my chaps pocket...when I took it out and put it in the box it started unfolding itself and flattened out...I would fold it or crease it and lay it down and watch it. It was kind of weird."

Brazel said that he showed the material to his father and his father said, "That looks like some of that contraption I found."

Brazel showed that small piece of foil to others. Sallye Tadolini was the daughter of Marian Strickland, one of Brazel's neighbors in 1947. She has the impression that the metal Brazel showed her was dull in color, maybe gray, and that it was a small piece. Brazel, according to her, balled it up in his hand and then opened his hand, letting it return to its original shape. She thought it was stiff, like aluminum foil but that it did not seem metallic.

Others around the Brazel ranch, such as Loretta Proctor saw a small "sliver" of the debris. It was a pencil sized piece that couldn't be cut with a knife or burned with a match. Proctor said that it looked like plastic but that she "didn't know what the stuff was."

Tommy Tyree said that he was riding with Brazel late in the summer when they spotted a piece of debris floating on top of the water in a sinkhole. Brazel told him it was a piece of the debris from the crash. Something light enough to float on top of the water. This, by itself, proves nothing since that debris could have been part of Mogul. What it does is establish that the military did not recover every scrape of material.

Military men picked up the debris for shipment from Roswell to various labs around the country. Robert Smith, an NCO with the 1st Transport Unit, told how he, along with a number of other men, loaded three or four aircraft with crates. All of them were large and many of them felt as if they were empty. Smith wasn't sure what was in them, but did say the loading took place under armed guard away from the main part of the ramp area at the airfield.

But Smith did learn what was in the crates. According to Smith, "We were talking about what was in the crates and so forth and he (another of the sergeants) said, 'oh, do you remember the story about the UFO?...We thought he was joking, but he let us feel a piece and stuck it back in his pocket."

Like all the others, Smith said, "It was just a little piece of metal or foil or whatever it was...It was foil-like, but it was a little stiffer than foil.. being a sheet metal man, that intrigued me, being that you could crumble it up and it would flatten back out again without any wrinkles showing up in it."

Henderson, one of the pilots who flew debris out of Roswell told a couple of friends about the debris. More importantly he apparently was in possession of a piece for a number of years. He showed it to a close friend, John Kromschroeder, who had an interest in metallurgy. Kromschroeder said that he had never seen anything like it.

The metal, according to Kromschroeder, was gray and resembled aluminum but was harder and stiffer. He could not bend it but had to be careful because the edges were sharp. He said that it didn't seem to have a crystalline structure and based this observation on the fracturing of it. He said it hadn't been torn.

Kromschroeder said that Henderson told him that the metal was part of the lighter material lining the interior of the craft. He said that when properly energized, it produced perfect illumination. It cast a soft light with no shadows.

That piece of debris apparently came from Major Ellis

Boldra. Boldra subjected the sample to a number of tests. It was thin, incredibly strong and dissipated heat in some matter. Boldra used an acetylene torch on the material, which didn't melt and barely got warm. It didn't glow when heated and once the flame was removed, it could be handled in seconds.

Boldra tried to cut it with a variety of tools and failed. No one remembers if he tried to drill through it. One of Boldra's friends said that it wasn't any type of metal that he could identify.

Boldra and Kromschroeder weren't the only ones to describe debris as incredibly strong. Lewis Rickett, the NCOIC of the counter intelligence office at Roswell had an opportunity to see some of the debris still on the impact site. By the time Rickett arrived, on July 8, the vast majority of the debris had been collected, but there were still some pieces scattered around.

According to Rickett, as he walked the field with Captain Sheridan Cavitt he wanted to know if it was "hot." He was told that there was no evidence of radioactivity.

Rickett found one piece that was about two feet square and crouched to pick it up. It was slightly curved but the only way he could tell that was to place it on something that was flat. He then locked it against his knee and used his arm to try to bend it. According to Rickett it was very thin and very light weight.

Cavitt said to Easley, "Smart guy. He's trying to do what we couldn't."

Rickett said the metal wasn't plastic and that it didn't feel like plastic but he had never seen a piece of metal that thin that couldn't be bent.

There are others who saw the debris. Glenn Dennis saw some of it in the back of the ambulances parked outside the base hospital. He described the debris as looking like "...the front part of a canoe...about three feet long...There were some inscriptions...going along the contour or the wreckage."

There were three types of debris that were consistently described by the witnesses. First, by far the most common, was the foil that was thicker than normal aluminum foil, more like a lead foil. But unlike either of those, this foil, when folded or wadded into a ball, would unfold itself with no sign of a crease. Witnesses to the foil include Bill Brazel, Frankie Rowe, Jim Ragsdale, Sallye Tadolini, and Robert Smith.

Second, Bill Brazel talked of the light weight material that reminded him of balsa wood but that was so strong that it couldn't be cut. Loretta Proctor handled something with similar properties. Rickett, Marcel, and Easley talked of light weight material, "as thin as newsprint" that could not be bent or marked.

Finally there were the wire like pieces that Bill Brazel described as flexible. He said that he could shine a light in one end and it would come out the other no matter how he twisted the wire around. This sounds suspiciously like fiber optics.

These are the eyewitnesses who saw or handled the debris found on either the debris field or the impact site. Dozens of people saw the material and who describe it in the same terms over and over. These remains are not the stuff of balloons, experimental aircraft or rockets. If, for example, the lead gauge foil could be made into something stronger, and it was Jesse Marcel's opinion that it was used to make the I-beams, then it could be used in the manufacture of automobiles. The next fender bender could be resolved by the drivers backing up and letting the metal return to its former shape.

The point is that no such material exists today. There is, after a fashion, molecules with a memory, but nothing that can be twisted out of shape and then return when the pressure is released.

The question becomes, who was making material with such strange properties? Why isn't there a hint of that material anywhere today?

The Craft and Bodies

Of course, this argument overlooks another massive block of eyewitness testimony and that is the descriptions of the craft and the alien bodies found on the impact site.

Ragsdale described a craft stuck in the ground at about a thirty-five or forty degree angle. Not a deflated balloon, not the remnants of some kind of a target device suspended under a balloon, but a craft of some kind. With that sort of eyewitness testimony, available for the first time, it seems that the balloon explanation, all of them from the rawin target balloons to a Japanese Balloon Bomb to a Project Mogul device can finally be eliminated.

If Ragsdale was alone in the description, there might be room for interpretation of it. But others who were on the impact site have corroborated Ragsdale's eyewitness account.

John McBoyle, a news man with radio station KSWS in Roswell was in a cafe in Roswell and overheard a conversation among some of the archaeologists. McBoyle convinced them to show him the location of the crash. The only description of it that McBoyle ever gave, confirmed in an interview conducted just prior to his death in 1992, was that there was an object that looked like "a crushed dishpan." An object about twenty-five to thirty feet long, impacted in a slope.

Kaufmann, one of the men on the site took his description of it farther, saying that it had a bat-like wing on it and that the front was crushed. It was stuck in the ground at an angle, suggesting that the forces at impact had been tremendous.

Another military officer, reviewing the files, reported that the craft was not of American manufacture and that it had a "scalloped wing." The object was no more than thirty feet long, had a fat fuselage and had hit the ground with an incredible force.

Major Edwin Easley, the provost marshal at Roswell, who was on the impact site, and who, in fact, was responsible for maintaining the cordon, said that the object had not been manufactured on Earth. When asked if pursuing the extraterrestrial theory was right, Easley confirmed that it was the right path.

Rickett, who was on the impact site after the main body of the craft had been removed said the same thing. The material he saw was from something that hadn't been made on Earth. Just days prior to his death, he said the object had been heel-shaped, using the same words as other first-hand witnesses.

The point is, the eyewitnesses, the men who were there, who were responsible for maintaining the security on the impact site, who were responsible for the retrieval of the craft and the bodies, all said the same thing. This was not a conventional aircraft manufactured on Earth.

Of course, the idea that it was an experimental craft disappears with the final piece of evidence. There were five bodies on the crash site. They were not human bodies, but alien creatures .

While it might be possible to argue the points about the metallic debris, to suggest that the witnesses were exaggerating, that the metal wasn't as impressive and therefore could be of advanced design, when the discussion returns to the bodies, the conventional explanations are eliminated. Metal is metal and wires are wires but there is no way to explain the bodies in the conventional.

When the investigation began, the rumors about bodies were little more than that. There was Barney Barnett who might have seen something, a hint of archaeologists on the site, but no solid, first-hand testimony. That objection has been eliminated.

Kaufmann made it clear that the bodies, though being more human in appearance than reported in other UFO sightings, they still were not human. They were smaller than human and they were thinner than human. Their eyes were slightly larger than human eyes. Kaufmann got close enough to examine them carefully.

Ragsdale also saw the bodies on the impact site. He couldn't provide details, except to say that he thought they might be dummies. They didn't look human and he wasn't thinking in terms of beings from outer space on the morning of July 5.

Easley was reluctant to talk of bodies, but finally, before he died, said that he had seen the creatures. He had been close enough to know they weren't human. He called them creatures.

It should be remembered that Easley, as the provost marshal, would have been responsible for cordoning aircraft crash sites during his tour in Roswell. The 509th Bomb Group, because of the number of flying hours it obtained, crashed a number of aircraft. Easley was on those sites as well. He had seen human bodies after they had been exposed to the forces of an aircraft accident and after they had been burned. Had the remains been those of a human, or humans, Easley would have recognized them as such. Instead, he said, "Oh, the creatures."

That is the problem with the theories that are all too often given. They do not take into account all the testimony from all the eyewitnesses. There is a new theory, for example, that the bodies seen on the impact site were chimpanzees. The idea is that the men were so caught up in the excitement of the moment, and that because of the time frame, meaning 1947, they wouldn't have recognized the bodies as belonging to animals, and that later, as theories about the extraterrestrial nature of the crash was discussed, they had "altered" their memories so that the apes, seen under bizarre circumstances became alien beings. After all, the men at Roswell wouldn't have expected to see chimpanzees in silver flight suits, so they assumed they were from another world.

The documentable evidence suggests that no primates were used in experimentation prior to 1948. The first monkeys, according to *Mercury Primates* by Gregory P. Kennedy, were launched on a V-2 rocket on June 11, 1948. These were not chimpanzees but small monkeys, not much larger than a house cat.

"The opportunity," according to Kennedy's report, "to place a live passenger...was presented two months before the planned flight...By using all the space available in the capsule, it was possible, with difficulty, to place a 9 pound rhesus monkey in it."

That is interesting for another reason. There are those who believed that it was possible that the Roswell crash was the result of a V-2 with two chimpanzees on board. But the records show that chimpanzees would have been much too large.

A search of the records fails to produce any suggestion that chimps were used in aviation or rocket research, either by the United States or the Soviet Union in the proper time frame. Those records suggest that use of chimpanzees by the American space program began in the 1950s and by the Soviets later. Chimpanzees, as the flight crew, has been effectively ruled out.

Of course the testimony of those on the impact site also rules it out. The face of a chimpanzee is distinctive. The eyes are small, not larger than a human's, the facial features are not fine, and there is thick hair on the head. The head itself is not proportionally larger than a human head on a human body. In other words, the descriptions of the bodies do not fit, even in the most liberal interpretation that of a chimpanzee or any other primate.

And finally, there are the archaeologists. These were men trained in the recognition of primates. While it could be argued, though ineffectively, that the officers at Roswell wouldn't have recognized the chimps, such an argument fails to explain why the archaeologists would have been fooled. There was no description from them that suggests the bodies were of chimps.

What we are left with then, is a large body of eyewitness testimony to the high strangeness of the debris. Thin metal of extraordinary strength, foil that unfolds itself assuming its original shape, strands of "wire" that sound like fiber optics, and I-beams that flex. No one has been able to demonstrate a single example of this material from that time frame. The properties described are unique.

While it is true that metal is metal and wire is wire, and there are always rumors of classified materials that can match those descriptions, when the conversation turns to the bodies, the debate ends. There is no way to explain them. Without eyewitness testimony, it could be suggested that the bodies were the figments of imagination. But the testimony of Kaufmann, Ragsdale, Easley, Holden, Gonzales and others eliminates that. One of them might be lying, but not all of them about the same thing. And the opportunities for missed identification fall off as well. Too much of the testimony corroborates their stories.

Were There Threats?

But the real proof is the reaction of the men assigned to bury the story. It is clear that they were trying to hide something that was extremely sensitive. They went out of their way to make sure that the civilian witnesses did not talk.

Grace Maurer, of Laurens, Iowa found what she thought was the story of the century when she was informed that a Japanese Balloon Bomb had landed in Iowa. She wrote her story but didn't publish it until the Second World War had ended. She sat on the article, not because the government had threatened her but because the FBI had visited and asked her not to publish. Maurer complied because she was convinced that it was her patriotic duty not to publish. No threats, no intimidation, no suggestion of prisons, but a request to remain silent.

Two years later, when something crashed at Roswell, the civilian witnesses were not asked to remain quiet, they were ordered to do so. Children, seven and twelve years old were confronted by armed soldiers who made threats. Frankie Rowe was told she would be taken into the desert and no one would see her again.

Glenn Dennis, at twenty-two was older but the treats no less vivid. He was told, first by an officer at the base hospital that they would be picking his bones out of the sand, and then by an NCO that he would make good dog food. To insure his silence, the military visited his family, as did the local sheriff. They didn't want him talking about the crash.

The sheriff himself, according to his granddaughter was threatened. If he told anyone what he had seen, he would be killed, as would his wife and his children. Not a veiled threat, but an overt threat designed to make sure that nothing leaked into the rest of the civilian community.

If the Roswell crash was the result of a secret American project, why were these people intimidated they way they were? No other project, with the possible exception of the Manhattan Project received that sort of treatment. Reviewing the records of the time, there is nothing that was happening that was so highly classified. In fact, in the weeks that followed the Roswell crash, the government revealed a number of balloon projects that had been classified until then. The implication was that the flying discs and the crash at Roswell were explainable by those balloons and those explanations. If read carefully many of these reports refer to the top secret Project Mogul.

There is no justification for the threats made to civilians. Again, we have good, first-hand testimony of those threats. Not from a single source, but from multiple sources. There is no doubt that the threats were made.

Those sorts of threats do not fit. If Grace Maurer had published her story of the balloon bomb in central Iowa, and the Japanese learned that bombing attacks were meeting with some success, then the war effort could have been hampered. Additional lives could have been lost. But even with that, a real danger, the FBI requested her assistance. At Roswell, the government demanded it.

If all the testimony about the strange qualities of the debris is ignored, if all the eyewitness testimony to the bodies is ignored, and even if all the failed attempts to explain Roswell in the mundane is ignored, there still remains that one glowing question. What was so important about the crash that the government had to threaten its own citizens to make sure they never mentioned it? What could be so important that the threats and intimidation continues? And if Roswell wasn't extraterrestrial, then just what was it?

Could It Have Been Project Mogul?

All the testimony seems to suggest that something other than a Project Mogul balloon was recovered on the Brazel ranch. There is additional information that underscore that fact, the Air Force opinion to the contrary.

First it must be remembered that the Air Force claims that Launch No. Four, made on June 4, 1947 is responsible for the debris. They imply in their report that these balloons were something special. In fact, polyethylene, a material that was in invented in 1947 might have fooled some of the less sophisticated witnesses because of its very nature. However, the records show that the first of the polyethylene balloons were not launched until July 3, 1947 and therefore couldn't have been found on the Brazil ranch.

Balloon Launch No. 4 was of a cluster of regular meteorological balloons made of neoprene rubber. The records show that this was part of the early flights to train the Watson Lab people so that they would be better able to track the balloons. It did contain a "sonobuoy" or microphone, but no "official" record was kept because no data of scientific importance was recovered. Charles Moore, one of the Mogul scientists said that they had lost track of Launch No. 4. He believed that it had disappeared near Arabela, New Mexico which is twenty or thirty miles south of the Brazel ranch site. Unfortunately there is no documentation to support this.

The other important point, though the Air Force does not make it clear, is that there was nothing special about the balloons in Launch No. 4. There was nothing on it that would fool anyone. They were standard balloons, about 15 feet in diameter, and made of rubber. Rubber that, after exposure to sunlight, would turn from a tan to a black. The color wouldn't be uniform. The portions directly exposed to sunlight would blacken faster than those in shadow. The point is that the rubber reacted to the heat and light from the sun. Attempts to cut it, or to burn it, would have been successful. And surely someone, if not Marcel himself, would have recognized the material as having come from a neoprene weather balloon.

The Air Force maintains that the balloon laid in the field from more than a month. *The Roswell Daily Record* suggests that Brazel found the balloon first on June 14, ten days after the launch, but left it there from another three weeks. This is in conflict with what ranchers have told us.

According to them, this sort of debris is not left on the pastures because the livestock would ingest it. They wouldn't search out the debris but would eat it. That sort of debris could kill the animals and a rancher wouldn't leave it where the livestock could get at it. If Brazel had found it on June 14, he would have picked it up on June 14. The only reason to report otherwise was to provide explanation for what Marcel and Cavitt found on July 7.

The Air Force also implies that the reason there was a cover up was to protect Project Mogul. While the project itself was highly classified, the balloons, rawin targets, and other equipment was not classified. There was little of intelligence value to be recovered by Soviet agents if they knew that balloons were being launched from the Alamogordo Army Air Field.

In fact there was so little of importance attached to the balloons that a story about them was published in the *Alamogordo News*. If Soviet agents were interested in Mogul and balloon launches, that article provided more than enough clues for them. There are photos of the balloon clusters, but more importantly, Watson Laboratories and some of the men involved in Mogul are mentioned.

Had what Brazel found been nothing more than a weather balloon, there would have been no reason for the elaborate events that took place around it. Brazel would have recognized it and disposed of it without having to consult the local sheriff or with the military at the base.

If it was only a weather balloon, as Sheridan Cavitt now claims, why didn't he mention it to anyone, saving the 509th from the embarrassment of announcing they had a flying saucer, only to have that statement challenged by the officers at the Eighth Air Force.

No, Project Mogul, although highly classified, does

nothing to explain the events on the Brazel ranch. There is too much testimony from too many military officers that suggest something else was going on there. Even if we accept the Mogul explanation, as pointed out, it does not explain the testimony of a second site, or of a specific craft and bodies.

Conclusions

The Air Force announced in 1947 that the explanation for the debris found at Roswell was a balloon. They maintained that answer for more than forty years and then decided to review the situation. They then announced that they had lied in 1947, and on a complete re-examination of the facts, interviews with the principals, they have discovered the truth about Roswell. It was...a balloon. Same answer and same balloon. It worked forty years ago. Why shouldn't it work today?

In their investigation, they didn't bother to interview anyone who would take them in a direction away from the single site at the Brazel ranch and the idea it was Project Mogul. They didn't interview Bill Brazel, Jr., Jesse Marcel, Jr., but did quote from affidavits that suggested the debris was nothing more than the remains of a Mogul balloon. They implied there was something special about the balloons, but in the end, the documentation shows the balloons were nothing more than common meteorological devices, easily recognized by civilians, military officers, and weather forecasters. They were so unspectacular, the material so flimsy that the repeated stories of its unusual properties must be referring to something else.

The Air Force reports that they believe that the debris was the remains of Launch No. 4, but they have no documentation to back up that conclusion. It might have come down on the Brazel ranch, but then it might not. Launch No. 4 was so unimportant that the Mogul staff didn't try to find it, though with later launches they did chase the balloons.

They said they found no evidence that anyone was sworn to secrecy and in fact, print the statement from Sheridan Cavitt that he was not. In the course of the interview with Cavitt, Colonel Weaver, an Air Force investigator, makes it clear that he has read both *The UFO Crash at Roswell* and *The Truth about the UFO Crash at Roswell.* In both I report that Major Edwin Easley, when first contacted about the events of July 1947 said, "I can't talk about it. I was sworn to secrecy." The Air Force, afraid of that statement, never asked about it and never challenged me on it. They ignored it because of the danger behind it.

When all the evidence is examined, we learn that there were more than just the three witnesses to debris on the Brazel ranch, and we learn there was more than one site. We learn there are named witnesses to the craft and bodies, and we learn from an Air Force Brigadier General that he flew over both sites.

The Air Force, in the conclusion of their report, provided a number of reasons why there had been no mention of "alien" bodies by them. One of those conclusions, that no "alien" passenger had been launched in a Mogul balloon is ridiculous on the surface. To further reject the idea because there is disagreement among the UFO groups is also ridiculous. All agree that bodies were recovered in New Mexico, and that the bodies were taken out of the state. While the precise details might be in dispute, the basic and important facts are not.

Further, to suggest that the claims of those who saw the bodies "are often attributed to people using pseudonyms, is, at best, misleading. In our work we used one pseudonym because the witness feared, not retribution by the government, but a horde of other researchers demanding that he tell them the story too. When the name of a witness becomes known to the general public, there are those who want to verify it themselves. Walter Haut, the PIO at Roswell in 1947, tells of people arriving at his home unannounced. My one pseudonymous witness wanted to avoid this. Had the Air Force asked, I would have provided the name as I did for CBS News.

Finally, to suggest that those making the biggest claims about alien bodies make their living from the "Roswell Incident" is a gross misrepresentation. Neither Don Schmitt nor I make our living off Roswell. We have, on the other hand, interviewed more than 500 people during more than two thousand interviews in our attempt to learn the truth. We have interviewed everyone of the witnesses to whom the Air Force spoke with the exception of Dr. Spilhaus. We had no agenda when we began. Can the Air Force investigators make a similar claim?

The Air Force has now tried the same explanation they used forty years ago. It is amazing that anyone would listen to it now, especially when it is remembered they didn't interview very many of the witnesses. They set out to prove an answer and satisfied themselves. That isn't investigation, it isn't science, but it is propaganda.

George "Jud" Roberts said that his broadcast license was threatened by officials in Washington, D.C.
Photo courtesy Kevin D. Randle

Who Was at the Brazel Ranch and Other Questions

A crucial question to understanding the Roswell case is who was on the Brazel ranch during that critical July 4 weekend. New theories about the crash coming from various researchers and the Air Force suggest the debris found by Brazel was nothing more than a balloon from the top secret Project Mogul. For this theory to work, we must accept some of the data from the newspapers, some of the testimony from those who were involved, and we must reject other data that do not fit this construct. In other words, we must select the data that we want to believe and eliminate that which we do not want to believe. We must twist the data to fit the theory rather than create a theory that fits all the data available.

To understand the problems with the testimony about who was on the ranch and who was at the ranch house, we must examine all the facts beginning with the tale told by Bessie Brazel Schreiber, daughter of Mac and who was fourteen in the summer of 1947. According to her, as reported in *The Roswell Incident* by Charles Berlitz and William L. Moore she had been with her father at the ranch when he found the debris field in early June. She described seeing "...so much debris scattered over the pas-

John Price of Roswell's UFO Enigma Museum at 6108 South Main, has been investigating the crash for years. Price and Don Ecker were the first to interview Thomas Gonzales, another first-hand witness to the events.

Photo courtesy Kevin D. Randle

tureland. There was what appeared to be pieces of heavily waxed paper and sort of aluminum-like foils. Some of these pieces had something like numbers and lettering on them, but there were no words that we were able to make out. Some of the metal-foil pieces had a sort of tape stuck to them, and when these were held to the light they showed what looked like pastel flowers or designs. Even though the stuff looked like tape it could not be peeled off or removed at all. It was very light weight but there sure was a lot of it."

In describing the lettering, Bessie Brazel, said, "...It looked like numbers mostly...They were written out like you would numbers in columns to do an addition problem. But they didn't look like the numbers we use at all."

So Bessie Brazel is claiming to have seen the debris, and in a July 9 article published in the *Roswell Daily Record,* that claim is reinforced. In fact, according to that article, Brazel was on the ranch with his wife, young daughter and son when he found the debris about the middle of June.

Bessie Brazel, however, mentions that she went with him to Roswell to talk to the sheriff. Again, according to *The Roswell Incident,* "We were with him in Roswell but we didn't go with him to see these people...They talked to Dad all day. The following day we were descended upon by military people and news people."

Bill Brazel, also quoted in *The Roswell Incident,* disagreed with Bessie's memory, saying, "Dad was in the ranch house with the two younger kids...next day he rounded up the two kids and took off for Roswell by way of Tularosa, where he stopped off and left the kids with Mother."

Jason Kellahin, a reporter for the Associated Press stationed in Albuquerque in July 1947 reported that after he received the call from AP headquarters in New York, that he, with Robin Adair, drove to Corona and out to the Brazel ranch. In his affidavit prepared by the Fund for UFO Research, Kellahin claims, "Our first stop was the Foster ranch, where the discovery had been made. At the ranch house, we found William "Mac" Brazel, his wife, and his small son. It was Brazel who made the find in a pasture some distance from the house."

Kellahin then claims, "Brazel took Adair and me to the pasture where he made his discovery. When we arrived, there were three or four uniformed Army officers searching some higher ground about a quarter of a mile away."

Kellahin also pointed out that Adair, who had accompanied him from Albuquerque, took photographs of Brazel and the balloon out in the field. In Kellahin's statement, he said, "Adair also took photos of Brazel and the debris at the ranch, but these were never used."

By way of contrast, Brazel's closest neighbors in 1947 were the Proctor's, Floyd and Loretta. According to them, Brazel was alone at the ranch house in July 1947, the family residing in Tularosa. In fact, Loretta suggests that her young son, William, known as Dee, was with Mac Brazel on the morning he found the debris field. It was when Mac escorted young Proctor back to his family that he showed them some small samples of the material spread in his pasture.

In personal interviews with Bill Brazel conducted by Don Schmitt and me, beginning in February 1989, he said nothing about the family being at the ranch house near Corona. According to him there was no electricity and no plumbing. When he read an article about the events in Roswell in an Albuquerque newspaper, he knew that his father needed help. In fact he said that he knew no one would be at the ranch, so he needed to get down there. When he arrived, on Saturday or Sunday the following weekend, no one was home. His father returned two or three days later.

The Stories Conflict

How do we resolve this dilemma? We have a body of evidence that suggests that Mac Brazel wasn't alone when he found the debris, and we have other evidence that suggests the family was in Tularosa and Brazel was with the neighbor's son. We have descriptions of the debris and the metal that almost match those provided by others. We have a date that does not conform at all.

What is the most accurate representation of the truth? Can we draw any sort of intelligence conclusion with all the data being offered?

We can draw some valuable and accurate conclusions by looking at the whole picture and examining it carefully. We will find conflicting testimony and will have to reject some of it. If we do not, then the story becomes so confusing that it will be impossible to understand it. However, we can't reject testimony just because we don't like it. We must present carefully throughout reasons for the acceptance of some testimony and the rejection of other. Without solid information and reasoning, our theories are no more valid than those rejecting testimony because it doesn't fit their framework of the case.

First, if we examine the entire story reported in the July 9 issue of the *Roswell Daily Record,* we learn that Brazel supposedly found the debris in mid-June. Karl Pflock, according to *Roswell in Perspective,* rejects the date as wrong, but then accepts the remainder of the story as accurate, including the description of the debris which is at odds with the testimony of so many first-hand witnesses including Jesse Marcel, Sr., Jesse Marcel, Jr., Bill Brazel, Loretta Proctor, Sallye Tadolini, and Lewis Rickett among others.

The July 9 Article

There are, however, other questions that arise from a close reading of the story. For example, Brazel said that on June 14, "about 7 or 8 miles from the ranch house...they came upon a large area of bright wreckage made of rubber strips, tinfoil, a rather rough paper and sticks." According to the newspaper, at the time, Brazel wanted to finish his rounds and didn't pay attention to it. But, on July 4, he mentioned it to the family and they all, Vernon, his young son, Bessie (misidentified in the newspaper as Betty) and wife went back to the spot to gather up the debris.

According to the newspaper story, "The next day he first heard about the flying disks, and he wondered if what he had found might be the remnants of one of these.

"Monday he came to town to sell some wool and while here he went to see Sheriff George Wilcox and 'whispered kinda confidential like' that he might have found a flying disk."

Wilcox called the air field and Major Jesse Marcel and a man in "plain clothes" accompanied Brazel home. They collected all the debris and "tried to make a kite out of it, but could not do that and could not find any way to put it back together so that it would fit."

Interestingly, in the article, there is a description of a balloon. According to Brazel, he didn't see the object in the air, nor did he see it before it was torn apart. He thought, according to the newspaper, "...it might have been as large as a table top. The balloon which held it up, if that was how it worked must have been about 12 feet long...the rubber was smoky gray in color and scattered over an area about two hundred yards in diameter.

"When the debris was gathered up the tinfoil, paper, tape and sticks made up a bundle about three feet long and 7 or 8 inches thick while the rubber made a bundle about 18 or 20 inches long and about 8 inches think... There were no words to be found anywhere on the instrument although there were letters on some parts of it. Considerable scotch tape and some tape with flowers printed upon it had been used in the construction...No strings or wire were to be found but there were some eyeholes in the paper to indicate some sort of attachment may have been used."

Brazel finished the interview saying, "I am sure what I found was not any weather observation balloon...But if I find anything else besides a bomb they are going to have a hard time getting me to say anything about it."

Let's look at this newspaper report one section at a time. First is the date. If we accept the June 14 report as accurate, then, clearly, Pflock's Mogul Balloon Launch No. 9 explanation fails because there are no missing flights in that time frame. All other Mogul Balloons are accounted for. Of course, the Air Force has selected a different flight, No. 4 as their explanation.

However, that date raises other questions. Why, for example, did Brazel forget about the balloon until July 4? Why did he mention on that day, and why did the family travel to the "crash-site" to pick up the debris then? In fact, Brazel knew nothing of the flying disks, according to the newspaper, until the day after they recovered the debris.

There is another point that no one has made. Brazel wouldn't have left the debris in the field for more than two weeks because the live stock would have eaten it. Veterinarians routinely travel to ranches to remove the metal and other debris from cattle stomachs. Leaving that debris scattered only invited trouble with the live stock.

Bill Brazel reports that his father wouldn't have been in Roswell in July to sell wool. That was done by contract and the purchaser of the wool came to the ranch, often employing his own people to sheer the sheep.

As mentioned, the description of the material, and of the debris field, does not match that provided by others including Jesse Marcel, Sr. Marcel said that it was two to three hundred feet wide and more than three-quarters of a mile long. Bill Brazel said there was a gouge about five hundred feet long through the center of it. That report was confined by Brigadier General Arthur Exon who reported to have seen the gouge. As did Robin Adair who said that he had flown over two distinct crash sites on his way to Roswell from El Paso.

Bill Brazel, among others, have mentioned that his father was alone at the ranch in July 1947. According to him, the family lived in Tularosa so that the youngsters could attend school. While school would have been out of session in July, it appears that the family was still living in Tularosa. The ranch house where Brazel stayed had no electricity or indoor plumbing. There was no easy communications with the outside world.

Bill Brazel makes one other point that is important. When read about his father in the Albuquerque newspaper, he knew that his father needed help on the ranch. He knew that no one would be there to take care of it. When he arrived, he found the place deserted.

All this brings about another question that seems to have eluded others. If Brazel's wife and kids were there, why would Brazel have to take them to Tularosa as mentioned in *The Roswell Incident*? And, if his wife was in Tularosa but not at the ranch, why would Brazel have to take the children so far out of his way? Why not just take them into Roswell? Brazel has no reason to suspect that anything of significance was going to happen in Roswell. All he knows is that he is going to tell the sheriff about the debris on his ranch.

Of course, if we believe the story, then the debris has

been picked up by Brazel and the family and he had no incentive to make the long drive into town. Unless it is something extremely unusual, or if there is so much of it that he can't get it all picked up.

Finally, Bessie Brazel said that she accompanied her father into town. If that is true, what happened to her? She said that she didn't accompany him to the sheriff, which doesn't seem all that impossible. However, Marcel, in all the interviews he granted before his death, never mentioned that Brazel had any children with him. Bessie Brazel apparently didn't return to the ranch with her father, and if that is the case, what happened to her?

We know, based on the testimony of others including Major Edwin Easley, 509th Provost Marshal, Marian Strickland, Loretta Proctor, and Bill Brazel, that Mac was held by the military for a number of days. If his wife and young children were at the ranch, why didn't anyone become concerned when Mac didn't reappear? He apparently left with Walt Whitmore, Sr. for a radio interview, but did not return for six to eight days. How come no one tried to find him?

What we can conclude from all of this is that the facts, as outlined in the article are in dispute. We can't use it to verify any other aspect of the case because it contains so many things that are wrong. Our best policy is eliminate it completely, finding it unreliable in too many aspects. What that means, simply, is that we don't use it as corroboration for that which we believe. Instead, we must search for that corroboration in other arenas, and when we find it, then we can be sure of our facts.

We must, therefore, reject the idea that Bessie Brazel, her mother and brother were at the ranch, based solely on the newspaper article. We have testimony from others who should have information, such as Bill Brazel and Mac's neighbors that lead to the conclusion that Mac was alone. And, if we accept this as valid, then anything that Bessie says about the case must be questioned in light of the failed corroboration for her involvement.

The Associated Press Reporters

Seeming corroboration for her tale comes from Jason Kellahin, the AP reporter dispatched from Albuquerque on July 8 to interview Brazel and to take photographs of him. Kellahin's tale, unfortunately, suffers from the same problems as does Bessie's. And, to make it worse, Kellahin has significantly altered his report from the first interviews, one conducted by Dr. Mark Rodeghier and a second conducted on video tape by me. Copies of the transcript of that interview, along with a copy of the tape, have been supplied to the Fund for UFO Research.

Kellahin told me, in an interview conducted on January 28, 1993 at his home, that he had received a call from the New York office of the Associated Press ordering him to Roswell on July 8. They, meaning Kellahin, and a technician, Robin A. Adair, drove to Vaughn, New Mexico, to a point just south of Vaughn where the Brazel ranch was located. "We had directions," he said.

The July 9 issue of the *Roswell Daily Record* told the story of Jason Kellahin and R.A. Adair, two AP men from the office in Albuquerque. They had been ordered to Roswell by the New York office to learn what they could about the events at Roswell and to send out wirephotos of Brazel. It was the first time that something like that had been attempted from Roswell. Reed Hatch, of the telephone company, had been told "to clear such circuits as were required for the operation and was also told to put on extra operators if the demand warranted."

Jason Kellahin remembered the story, although, he said that it was just like every other story he had been assigned. According to him, they received the report in the morning and headed down to Vaughn, New Mexico. There, or on one of the ranches near there, Kellahin received directions so that he could find the Brazel ranch. "We went down to Vaughn. Just south of Vaughn is where they found the material."

According to him, they left the highway and drove toward the west. They hadn't driven far from the main highway, using only a couple of back, gravel roads. The site they searched for was not far from Vaughn and they knew they had found it when the spotted a number of parked cars. "We got over there we saw a lot of cars and went over. We assumed that was the place. There were officers from the air force base. They were there before we got there." He made it clear under questioning that they did not drive out onto a field. They parked beside the road and walked to where the military officers were standing.

The cars were civilian, military and state police. There weren't many of them, maybe half a dozen, all pulled off to the side of the road. "There were cars there and the officers from the air base were there but they were down at the south end of the field we went into. We stopped and saw where the debris was laying on the ground. This man from Albuquerque with me, he had a camera. He took some pictures of the stuff laying on the ground and of the rancher who were there. Brazel I believe his name was. Brazel was there and he took his picture."

Kellahin talked to Brazel briefly, conducting a short interview but then the military stepped in. They escorted Brazel from the field and, according to Kellahin, "[T]he military took him on down to Roswell and I didn't get to talk to him until, I think, it was the next day."

While on the ranch, Kellahin examined the material that had been found. "It wasn't anything much. Just some silver colored fabric and very light wood...A light wood like you'd make a kit with...I didn't pick it up. In fact, they asked us not to pick up anything."

The debris, according to Kellahin, didn't cover a very big area. "A half acre maybe. You couldn't pick it up and have identified what it was. You have to had known. But it was a balloon. It looked more like a kite than anything else."

Kellahin made it clear that the military didn't interfere with him at all. "I went wherever I wanted to go. They didn't keep me off the place at all. Me or the photographer."

Kellahin stayed on the ranch for an hour or two, and then drove the rest of the way into Roswell. Kellahin does not remember much about that second interview of Brazel. "About the only thing he said he walked out there and found this stuff and he told a neighbor about it and the neighbors said you ought to tell the sheriff...[I] even think it was the next day he went down to Roswell to talk to the sheriff who told the military. That's all the information I had."

Kellahin prepared a story for the AP that night which appeared in the morning newspapers such as *Albuquerque Journal* on July 9 but was datelined July 8. That point would become significant later.

Kellahin's story outlined the situation including the three hours "Until Roswell Find Collapses." It contained the balloon explanation that had been offered by Warrant Officer Irving Newton in Fort Worth. The information was filtering out of Eighth Air Force headquarters.

On July 9, Kellahin and Adair were in the *Daily Record* office, setting up their equipment. Kellahin saw Brazel again but this time he was with three or four military officers. "I think the military was talking to him and wouldn't let him talk to anyone else."

They hooked up the machinery to transmit the pictures but by that time the story was dead. The excitement of the day before was gone with the official announcement. Since they were already there, they sent the pictures of Brazel and then packed up to drive back to Albuquerque.

Kellahin did interview the sheriff while in Roswell, but didn't get much from him. Kellahin said, "By that time the military had gotten into it. He was being very cautious." And, he didn't talk to anyone out at the base.

There are, however, a number of problems with Kellahin's story. Because he, like all reporters, left a written record, we can compare what he tells us today with what was written in July 1947 when the events were still fresh. And, because we have a larger view of the events, we can draw a few conclusions.

First, Kellahin said that he'd left for Roswell early on the morning of July 8. Although he couldn't remember the date, we can reconstruct it based on the timing of his articles and the dateline from the newspaper. Clearly he was in Roswell on July 8.

That means that he arrived there by the evening of July 8 and not on July 9. This is important because he said that he left early in the morning. There was, however, no reason for him to have left Albuquerque on the morning of July 8. There was no story in Roswell until Walter Haut, the public information officer of the 509th Bomb Group issued his press release. It is clear, based on what Haut recalls, what various other reporters and editors in Roswell remember, and other documentation, that the press release was not available before noon. The call from New York to the Albuquerque AP office, then, couldn't have arrived before noon, and Kellahin wouldn't have left for Roswell before noon.

Of course, getting to Roswell from Albuquerque was no real problem. There were paved roads, first from Albuquerque and then Highway 285 from the area now called Cline's Corners. Even in 1947, it was only a three or four hour drive. Given the situation, they could easily have arrived before dark, especially when it is remembered this was summer.

There is a problem, however, if he stopped at the Brazel ranch. Kellahin was quite clear that he had gotten the information about the ranch in Vaughn. He then left the highway south of Vaughn, didn't drive very far until he found the men in the field. At least that is what he told me on video tape.

However, the debris field is a long way from the Vaughn highway. It is almost twenty miles from Highway 285 along Highway 147 to the point where the dirt road intersects the highway. From there it is another twenty miles or more to the debris field. The real problem, however, is that the debris field is not close to a road. It is necessary to drive across the high desert to get there. Even if there had been military vehicles parked by the side of the road, there would have been a two or three mile walk proper area. And, given the lay of the land, there is no way to see it from the road.

If Kellahin's story is accurate, it would mean that the military "salted" the area with fake debris. Given the timing, and this is based on the documentation available and not the memories of the participants, the balloon that Kellahin claims to have seen could not be the debris that Brazel found. Again, the testimony and the documentation proves that the Brazel debris was already on its way to Fort Worth. The press release also said that the debris had been recovered, not that they were in the process of recovering it.

Based on all the evidence available, this is what we believe happened. Kellahin, during his interviews with us, made it clear that the story, as he had gotten it originally, wasn't very important to him. One minute it was the hottest of stories and the next it was yesterday's news and he was assigned something else. He saw nothing extraordinary and there was no reason for him to remember this event as extraordinary.

We know, having spoken to Kellahin, that he read the article he wrote and that he had read *The Roswell Incident* before the interviews. With that firmly in mind, he then reconstructed the events as he believed they would have happened. This is evident by his claim that they left Albuquerque early in the morning. Until the press release was issued there was nor reason for anyone to be interested in Roswell.

Kellahin said that he had a photographer with him and that he, the photographer, took a number of pictures of the balloon laying in the pasture. The question that must be asked is where are those pictures? Pictures of the alleged debris displayed in Fort Worth have been found. The pictures of Brazel, Wilcox, and others have been found. All were put on the AP wire and have been located in various newspapers around the county. But the pictures of the balloon on the ranch, pictures that would be more important than those taken in General Ramey's office, have not been located in a search of more than one hundred newspapers. A check with the Associated Press also failed to locate them. If those pictures existed, they would have been printed in the newspaper, just as the pictures of Jesse Marcel, George Wilcox, General Ramey, and even Warrant Officer Irving Newton were. Because the pictures haven't been found, it is reasonable to conclude that they do not exist and were never taken.

Obviously Kellahin and Adair received the telephone calls sometime after noon and made their way to Roswell. Kellahin's story of talking to people in Vaughn and learning the location of the ranch simply doesn't track especially when compared to what he says now. The location he gives, as well as the timing, is wrong. By the afternoon of July 8, Brazel was already in Roswell. He wasn't on the ranch.

Based on the documented evidence, that is, the articles that were published in the right time frame, we believe that Kellahin drove directly to Roswell. Once there, he went to the offices of the *Roswell Daily Record,* asked a few questions, but by that time, after 5:00 P.M., the story was already beginning to unravel. Ramey, in Fort Worth, along with members of his staff, had already announced that the find was nothing more than a weather balloon. That can be documented as early as 4:30 PM Roswell time. Rather than being the number one story in the country, it was slipping to just another front page story and finally slipped from the front page altogether. An answer had been offered and there seemed to be no one around who was contradicting it.

There were important questions to be asked. What did Mac Brazel say? Kellahin could only remember the statement that had been published in the newspapers of July 9 which was that if he found anything short of a bomb, he wasn't going to tell anyone. If Brazel said anything else to him, Kellahin has long forgotten.

In fact, that seems to be the key to this end of the investigation. We can reconstruct it because of the written record, but Kellahin has long forgotten about it. He tried to help us, did his best to remember, but in the end, we have nothing new to add to the case. During an investigation, sometimes that's the best that can happen.

There is one other consideration. Pflock, in his report, suggests the crash debris was part of a highly classified balloon project, yet Kellahin is allowed to roam freely and Adair, according to Pflock, is allowed to photograph the debris. Kellahin does not suggest the film was confiscated. Instead, it was just never printed. That simply makes no sense.

What this means is that Kellahin's testimony on the case is no more reliable than Bessie Brazel's. There is just too many things that don't match.

What it demonstrates, when compared with the testimony of others including Bill Brazel, Jesse Marcel, Sr., Loretta Proctor and Marian Strickland, is that Brazel was alone at the ranch when he found the debris. Bessie Brazel claims to have accompanied her father into Roswell, but no one ever reported her there. Marcel never mentioned that Brazel was accompanied by children. When interviewed, he was asked who else might be available, but never suggested that Brazel's children were involved. Bessie disappears in Roswell and then reappears on the ranch.

Based on all the evidence, and our conclusions drawn from all the eyewitness testimony, Mac Brazel was alone. The July 9 article was designed to weaken interest in the Roswell story, providing details that sounded as if he had found a weather balloon and did nothing about the discovery for more than three weeks.

Neither Kellahin nor Bessie were there to see the things they reported. Kellahin is honestly reporting what he believes to be the truth, but it has changed too radically, and it is at odds with too much of the record to be treated seriously now. Pflock mentions Adair in a footnote in his report, but rejects the testimony in a single line. He offers no solid reason for this rejection, other than he found it to be badly flawed.

To understand the Roswell case, we must reject the testimony of Bessie Brazel and Jason Kellahin. We must reject it for solid reasons, realizing that their stories can lead us down the wrong path. There is no evidence that what was found by Brazel was a balloon, especially when it is remembered how flawed some of the testimony is.

This explains why it is important to know who was at

the ranch in July 1947. If we don't, then we spend time chasing bad information.

Does "Reluctant" Make the Story Better?

Of course, that leaves one witness, unidentified by Pflock, but named "Reluctant," by him. Of Reluctant, Pflock writes, "...who for reasons I understand and respect wishes to remain anonymous for the time being." I know who it is, having interviewed him myself. I could identify him, but he asked to remain anonymous. Although others delight in naming those who requested they not be named by anyone, I will respect "Reluctant's" request although he made no such request of me. Isn't too bad that others don't respect the wishes of those interviewed. In fact, Kaufmann told Pflock, more than once, not to use his name in any way, shape, or form. Pflock ignored that request.

Describing the testimony of Reluctant, Pflock writes, "... Brazel sketched a map for me, showing which roads to take and how to find the site. I drove there alone...a distance of 65 or 70 miles. No was there when I arrived, I do not remember seeing any sign that anyone had been on the site...I am certain I was on the site before any military personnel got there."

According to Reluctant, "The site was a short distance from a ranch road. The debris covered a fan- or roughly triangle-shaped area, which was 10 or 12 feet wide at what I thought was the top end. From there it extended about 100 to 150 feet widening out to 150 feet at the base...The material was very light. I could see it blowing in the wind."

Reluctant, according to Pflock, described the material as "...white, linen-like cloth with reflective tinfoil attached to one side. Some pieces were glued to balsa wood sticks, and some of them had glue on the cloth side, with bits of balsa still stuck to it. Most of the pieces were no larger than four or five inches on a side, although I found one or two about the size of a sheet of typing paper. None of the sticks was more than a foot or so long."

Reluctant told Pflock, and he told me, that he had collected some of the material and brought it home. Pflock reports that Reluctant told him, "It is...stored in a safe and secure place." He told me that it had been in a safe deposit box, but now it was somewhere in his "junk room."

Those aren't the only statements made by Reluctant on the record. Although the source is less than sterling, Berlitz and Moore report in *The Roswell Incident* that Reluctant "...said that while he did not see the actual crash site until after the Army Air Force had 'cleaned it up,' he did see some of the wreckage brought into town by the rancher. His description was that it consisted mostly of a very thin but extremely tough metallic foil-like substance and some small beams."

Interestingly, Berlitz and Moore also report Reluctant telling them, "Some of this material had a sort of writing on it which looked like numbers that had been either added or multiplied. He recalls that his father went out of the site in a Buick but was turned back by armed MPs who had set up a road block."

Other aspects of Reluctant's statements to Pflock are corroborated by *The Roswell Incident*. According to the book, Reluctant "...ventured out to the site and found a stretch of about 175–200 yards of pastureland up-rooted in a sort of fan-like pattern with most of the damage at the narrowest part of the fan.

Reluctant also provided Berlitz and Moore with a description of the material. "...the largest piece of this material that he saw was about four or five inches square, and that it was very much like lead foil in appearance but could not be torn or cut at all. It was extremely light weight."

Comparing Reluctant's testimony to Berlitz and Moore with that given to Pflock, we see few changes. Today, however, Reluctant describes seeing the debris, but with Moore he only described seeing the remains of the clean-up effort. He mentioned seeing debris, but in the custody of the sheriff. I assume that is what he meant because the debris brought in by Brazel was kept at the jail.

Reluctant's description of the material, as detailed in the Berlitz and Moore book, is more consistent with that provided by others such as Marcel, Brazel, and Rickett, than it is with his later interviews. When I spoke to him, it was clear that he was describing something that sounded like the material used in balloon construction.

Of course, if we accept the Air Force explanation that it was Mogul Flight No. 4, that creates additional problems. First, there would have been no polyethelene for Reluctant to find because the polyethylene balloons had not arrived in New Mexico yet. The only documentation currently available suggests that Flight No. 4 was made of normal balloons and one sonobuoy so there was no metallic debris like that described by Reluctant to be found. In other words, if we follow the Air Force lead, the debris being described by Reluctant doesn't fit the facts that have been presented.

If, on the other hand, we accept Pflock's Flight No. 9, we still have a problem. According to the documentation and testimony currently available, there was no metallic debris to be found. Flight No. 9 was stripped of all the equipment including the rawin targets. Dr. C.B. Moore said that the flight was made up of meteorological balloons. Again, the debris described by Reluctant doesn't match that which would have been scattered by a balloon, even a top-secret Mogul balloon.

The real problem is that Reluctant's story has grown since he first told it to Moore. Reluctant told me that he had come home on vacation from law school in Denver for the long holiday. When he arrived, he found his room occupied by Mac Brazel. Early the next morning Brazel was awake and making coffee. Reluctant, awakened by the noise, joined Brazel in the kitchen and heard the story of the debris field. With a map, provided by Brazel, he drove out to the site.

If we attempt to put the pieces together, we learn that the only day Mac Brazel could have been at Reluctant's house is Monday, July 7. Prior to that, Brazel is on the ranch, and on Sunday he was in Roswell before leading Marcel back to the debris field. On July 8, after the story broke in the newspaper, it's clear that Brazel spent the night on the base.

The main problem, however, is the claim to having samples of the material. For more than two years he has promised to produce the debris, but has yet to do it. He says that it's in his junk room, somewhere, and it's just a matter of locating it. As mentioned, in two years, he's failed to find it.

Like Pflock's other witnesses, Reluctant's story is inconsistent with established facts, something that Pflock conveniently overlooks. But what this means is that the third leg of Pflock's support has been kicked loose. His whole theory is based, not on solid fact as he would have us believe, but on a flimsy structure that is already collapsing. With no evidence to support his Mogul launch no. 9, with his three witnesses contradicting themselves, with no corroboration for their stories, Pflock's theory must be rejected...for the time being.

The Air Force fairs no better. While they offer nothing to substantiate the balloon theory, they use it none the less. Flight No. 4 was no more responsible for the debris than Flight No. 9 or any of the Mogul balloons. There is simply no evidence for it.

Project Mogul balloons were launched from the Alamogordo Army Air Field which adjoins the White Sands Missile Ranch. Tracking of the balloons was done at sites also used to track the rocket flights from White Sands.

Photo courtesy Kevin D. Randle

A Few Points That Deserve Some Answers

In the course of his work to disprove part of the Roswell case, Pflock made many allegations against those who have claimed first-hand knowledge. The majority of these people were not witnesses who came forward, but people who were found by extensive investigation. By selecting the data used, by ignoring corroborative testimony, and by making statements that aren't backed by facts, Pflock has presented one side of the case. By adding the rest of the facts and by reviewing Pflock's work and the Air Force analysis, a different picture is drawn.

One UFO researcher wanted to know how those outside the main stream could determine the truth if various investigators could come to such diverse conclusions by interviewing the same witnesses. The answer is simple. The investigators must present as much data as they can and let the reader decide who is right. This is not a debate where we are trying to win points, but a search for the truth. To learn the truth, everything must be known otherwise we are left guessing about the situation.

Much of the information has been presented in other sections of this report. There are somethings that didn't fit into that structure, so they are discussed here. Once again, there is so much that is wrong in Pflock's report and the Air Force analysis, that only the high points are corrected

The Space Museum in Alamogordo where records, reports and documents relating to the early days of experimentation can be found.

Photo courtesy Kevin D. Randle

here. Documentation is supplied where appropriate.

Colonel Blanchard and His Controversial Leave

In the complex story that has become Roswell, there are often side issues that become momentarily important. One of these was the case of Gerald Anderson's phone bill and the length of his conversation with me. The length of the call, in and of itself, was trivial. It only became important when Anderson offered a telephone bill showing a conversation that did not match the length of the recording made by me. Without that bill, and Anderson's subsequent admission that he had constructed it, we might still be debating the validity of the Anderson story. It revealed something that was critical to understanding the Anderson testimony and where it fit into the scheme of the whole Roswell case.

There are other points that seem to be trivial when first encountered, but when brought to light take on great significance. Such is the question of when Colonel William Blanchard, commanding officer of the 509th Bomb Group went on leave. Pflock, in his report, suggests that Blanchard began his leave on July 9 instead of July 8 as I've insisted. The question of the actual date of the leave might seem to be of little or no importance, until the whole picture is examined.

Pflock writes, "According to the 509th's headquarters morning report and a tiny Associated Press story in the July 10 *Albuquerque Journal,* the ninth (not the eighth) was the day he began 'a three week leave in Santa Fe and Colorado.' ...he was on his way north on a long planned vacation..."

Pflock continues, writing, "Taken together, these admittedly fragmentary and in some part questionable bits of testimony and documentation point to a delay before the 509th was instructed to treat the Brazel discovery as a sensitive matter. They also suggest Blanchard may have personally conveyed this guidance to those in the field, perhaps as he was on his way north on a long—planned vacation—although some have contended he headed somewhere else entirely."

What this demonstrates is that Pflock has misunderstood the significance of Blanchard's leave and the timing of the events. In fact, when examined carefully, it becomes clear that the timing actually reinforces the theory that the 509th was involved in the situation before Mac Brazel arrived in Roswell with a box of debris on July 6.

The first part of Pflock's analysis is a question that can be resolved without debate, varied interpretation of eyewitness testimony or rancor. We can review the situation and draw a valid conclusion about it based on all the documentation currently available.

First, we have the eyewitness testimony from Lieutenant Colonel Joseph Briley. (According to the unit history and *UFO Crash at Roswell,* Briley became the Operations Officer in the middle of July. Prior to that, he had been a squadron commander.) Briley said Blanchard had gone to the crash site. From the information available, it seems that this visit was made on July 8 and that Blanchard's leave began on July 8. The leave was actually a cover for Blanchard's activities revolving around the crash.

Pflock uses the testimony of Robert Shirkey to refute this idea, writing, "It is entirely possible, even likely, Blanchard went to the debris field to survey the situation personally. However, reliable testimony suggests he did not do so the afternoon of July 8. First, according to Robert Shirkey, about mid-afternoon that day he was with Blanchard in the Roswell AAF operations building, where the colonel personally was overseeing the dispatch of the B-29 which took Jesse Marcel and some of the debris to Fort Worth. Second, Walter Haut vividly recalls Blanchard colorfully complaining to him that same afternoon about not being able to place outside telephone calls because the base switchboard was tied up with inquiries about the flying saucer."

While this is interesting, it is not overly significant. It seems, according to other testimony, that the debris put on the aircraft arrived in Fort Worth about 4 PM local time, or 3 PM Roswell time. Newspaper articles and testimony from J. Bond Johnson suggests the debris was in Ramey's office about that time. It means, simply, that Blanchard was on the base at Roswell prior to the flight leaving, as much as an hour and a half before then (1:30 PM Roswell time) and then left for his leave. There is nothing contradictory in this and allows for both points to be correct.

Second, as Pflock suggests, the morning reports show that Blanchard was present for duty on July 8 but had signed out on leave before the morning report was created on July 9. These documents are available from the Army in St. Louis and I recovered a complete set of the headquarters morning reports (which were indirectly supplied to Pflock) from 1 June to July 31, 1947 through the use of the Freedom of Information Act.

This too, does not contradict the belief that Blanchard went on leave on July 8. If Blanchard signed out on leave in the afternoon of July 8, then the morning report would show him present on the eighth and gone on the ninth. Which is exactly what it does show.

The newspaper article quoted by Pflock is interesting, but probably irrelevant. It is, after all, a newspaper article, and it shows, again, that Blanchard was gone on the ninth, but not when he signed out from the base.

The critical piece of evidence is General Order Number 9, issued by Headquarters, 509th Bomb Group and dated July 8, 1947. It says, "Pursuant to the authority contained in Hqs. 8th Air Force TWX number Al 1593 dated 6 July 1947, the undersigned hereby assumes command of the Roswell Army Air Field, Roswell New Mexico. Effective this date." It was signed by Payne Jennings, Lt. Col. A.C. (Air Corps), commanding.

This then, is the definitive proof. Jennings assumed command on the eighth. It means that Blanchard went on leave on the eighth. If Blanchard went on leave on the ninth, as Pflock suggests, then the general order would reflect that. Eighth Air Force wouldn't want to create a situation where there were two commanders on station at the same time.

But there are other points that must be made. What the general order does is show military interest in the case days before July 8. It shows that Blanchard's leave was not long planned because the TWX was sent on July 6, a Sunday. Had it been a long-planned leave, the TWX would have been sent earlier. If it was a long-planned leave, there was no reason to wait until Sunday, July 6 before sending the TWX. That date only becomes important when it is placed in the context of all the activities of that critical weekend.

In fact, we can see that the military was interested in the case, not by Mac Brazel's arrival, for had that been the reason, nothing would have happened on July 6. Brazel arrived with debris that was interesting, but, if we follow the conventional wisdom, that is all it is, until Jesse Marcel, and Sheridan Cavitt return late on July 7. If the headquarters had waited for that, and for the cursory examination of the debris on the morning of July 8, then the documents would have been dated that way. The TWX demonstrates the military was interested prior to July 8.

It might be suggested that the TWX and the general

order are a result of the rumors in Roswell. The military officials, both in Roswell and Fort Worth, probably in consultation with those in Washington, realized that it would be necessary for Blanchard to monitor the activities. The problem was, after the story began to leak, Blanchard's absence would have been noticed by the news media. Without Brazel's arrival, and the rumors spreading through Roswell, there would be no reason to cover Blanchard's absence and to grant him leave.

It leads to another point, one that wasn't lost on the military planners. If the story was so important, if it involved a "real flying saucer," would Blanchard leave the base? Surely the commanding officer of the 509th would not want to be off the base and out of town when the biggest event of the 20th Century took place unless his leave itself was part of the cover-up.

On the other hand, if it was nothing more than a weather balloon, as the military announced, then the absence of the commander wouldn't matter. Blanchard wouldn't be expected to cancel his leave over something as trivial as a crashed weather balloon.

So the TWX, on July 6 becomes as important as the general order because it demonstrates what was happening inside the military. They were responding to the events of the day before. They were preparing for what was coming. The TWX on July 6 suggests that the military knew what was happening on the sixth, and they knew that because of what had been found on the impact site by military officers on July 5.

We have to examine one other aspect of this case. By July 8, when the press was interested in the Roswell case, the key players had been removed. Mac Brazel was in military hands, held in the guest house at the base according to Major Edwin Easley, the 509th Provost Marshal. Jesse Marcel, the only man mentioned by name in the press release, is no longer in Roswell, but on his way to Fort Worth, or already there and insulated by the commander of the 8th Air Force, Brigadier General Roger Ramey. And Colonel Blanchard? Why, he's on leave, heading to the north and into Colorado.

There are other facts that lead to this conclusion. Ignoring the testimonies of both Frank Kaufmann and Jim Ragsdale who describe activities on the impact site during the recovery of the craft and bodies, we can still provide testimony to the 509th's involvement prior to the July 8 press announcement. Leo Spear, an MP in Roswell in July 1947 reported that he had no direct knowledge of the situation. All he knew was that other MPs returned to the barracks talking about the crashed flying saucer. Spear, like the others who had not been used as guards, thought they were "BS-ing." But, according to Spear, when they read about the saucer in the newspaper (July 8), a day or two after he'd heard about it from his fellow MPs, he changed his mind.

The key to that is that he'd heard about the crash from the guards prior to the press release. It was the release that convinced him there was something to their story. This corroborates the reports of those who claim military involvement on July 5, and supports the idea that the military was preparing for contingencies on July 6. It suggests they knew a great deal more much earlier than researchers have believed until recently.

All of this refutes Pflock's theories about Blanchard's leave and when he took it. It shows that Pflock drew his conclusions without having reviewed all the important documents or testimonies. It also shows that the military was active in the Roswell case on July 5 and that they were planning for all contingencies on July 6 by, among other things, putting Blanchard on leave.

What we can do is restructure the time line based on

the testimony of the participants and underscore the validity of those changes with the documentation that exists. The old time line suggested no military interest until Mac Brazel arrived. After all, how could the military begin a recovery before they knew there had been a crash?

The answer is, they didn't. They knew of the crash on July 5 and began the recovery then. Blanchard's leave is the key to understanding this. First, we have to ask, why would anyone begin a leave on a Tuesday afternoon? Or, even is we accept Pflock's analysis, why begin on a Wednesday?

An exception would be made for an emergency leave but that doesn't seem to be the case. Nothing in the documentation shows that Blanchard was responding to a personal emergency such as a very sick family member. Based on the fragmentary documentation he produces, Pflock concludes the leave was routine.

The circumstances, and the General Order No. 9, refutes that, showing the military responding to a critical situation. Blanchard's leave was not routine, but it was not an emergency leave in the normal sense. They were freeing Blanchard to respond to the situation as necessary without having to worry about awkward questions from the media.

What we have is more support for the new time line. It demonstrates the military involvement and their planning prior to Mac Brazers arrival on July 6. To understand what was happening, we must examine all the evidence in a dispassionate light. When we do, we see how all the facts fit into a complete whole without gaps in the knowledge. We are not forced to twist the material to make it fit, nor are we forced to omit material for our theory to work.

It is clear, based on the evidence, that Blanchard began his leave on Tuesday, July 8 and that it wasn't long planned. It was a response to a situation that began on

July 5 when the military recovered a flying saucer just north of Roswell. It became critical when Mac Brazed found the debris field and reported it, not only to the military officers at the Roswell Army Air Field, but also to the local sheriff and a reporter for a local radio station. That is what all the documentation tells us .

We now understand this small segment of the Roswell case. It helps us understand the larger picture, and by doing that, gives us insight to the Roswell case. Little things, like Blanchard's leave can grow into important structures. Dealing with the trivia sometimes leads us to the proper conclusions. But do so, we must have all the evidence, not just some of it. And, we must understand the significance of that evidence. If we don't, then our conclusions will be faulty and unreliable.

Was There a Written Press Release?

Pflock creates another problem, suggesting that there had never been a written press release, but that Walter Haut had called the various news media on the phone. Pflock writes, "...George Walsh... unequivocally says Haut gave him the announcement over the telephone..." Later he quotes Walsh as saying, "He [Haut] also said, 'I got a call from the War Department that told me to shut up.' This was very unusual, so I asked him if the department had given him a correction or another contact to provide the media. He told me his orders were to quote, shut up, unquote."

Pflock continues, writing, "No copy of the release has ever been found, and although there are claims the reason for this is the Army rounded up and destroyed all copies, it seems more likely that, except perhaps for the copy Haut used, there was never a written release...It is very difficult to credit the idea that professional newsmen and press and public relations specialists such as George Walsh, Art

McQuiddy, and Jud Dixon would not have a vivid memory of the Army taking stormtrooper-style action against them."

But, once again, the situation isn't as black and white as Pflock makes it sound. As late as August 15, 1994 Walter Haut told a radio audience that he had hand delivered the press release to the four media in Roswell. At no time did he suggest that he might have called them rather than personally visiting them. Haut also confirmed, on that same program, that Frank Joyce had advised him, in person, not to make the release as it had been written just as Joyce has claimed for years.

In an interview conducted with Art McQuiddy on January 19, 1990, he told me, "I can remember quite a bit of what happened that day. It was about noon and Walter Haut brought in a press release. He'd already been to one of the radio stations."

McQuiddy also claims that he surrendered the press release to the military, saying, "As I recall, Walter didn't come in and ask to have the release back or anything although it sticks in my mind that he did, but he says that he didn't...I thought he did and said he says he didn't."

And, of course, Pflock does write that Frank Joyce tried to hide some of the paper to prove what had happened, but someone had made "sweep" of the station, collecting much of the paper that had been hidden. Apparently Pflock doesn't find this testimony credible and therefore ignores it.

One other point that must be made is that Walter Haut denies that he was ever called by the military or the Pentagon and berated for issuing the press release. Walsh may have read that claim in any of the various newspapers where it was alleged "Lieutenant Haught (sic) reportedly told reporters that he had been 'shut up by two blistering phone calls from Washington.'"

On April 20, 1989, I called Haut to ask him about the clipping (I had one from the July 9, 1947 issue of the *Las Vegas Review-Journal,* but have seen it in a dozen other newspapers). I asked if he remember anything like that. His answer was quick and clear. "Nope."

He did clarify, adding, "Well, I think that had I really gotten any calls from Washington, a first lieutenant getting calls from the big boys, I'd remember it."

What becomes apparent here is that a number of people, Walter Haut, Art McQuiddy, and Frank Joyce remember a written release but George Walsh doesn't. McQuiddy and Joyce remember the military retrieving the release, McQuiddy believing that it was Haut who retrieved it.

Pflock reports that Jud Dixon doesn't remember any sweep of paper or any sort of military attempt to recover any documentation that would add credibility to the case. Of course Pflock forgets to mention that Dixon was at the bureau office in Santa Fe, not in Roswell.

A very plausible explanation for the apparent discrepancies is that Walsh didn't see the physical press release so that he believes there might not have been one. The story that Haut received a "blistering rebuke" was well publicized at the time, but seems to be one more piece of the Army's well-oiled public relations machine but a fact not grounded in reality. Haut, himself, denies it.

When this is examined carefully, like most of the points that Pflock raises, we see that it is actually a problem of perspective. The differences between what Walsh said, and the others have said, isn't very great. There are simple explanations for the alleged discrepancies that revolve around, more than anything else, the point of view of the man being interviewed. In this case, none are lying or confabulating. They are merely reporting what they saw from their perspective. It is up to us to fit it into the framework of the Roswell case though when all is said and done, the point is, there was a written press release.

Frankie Rowe and the Truth

Pflock rejects the testimony of Frankie Rowe writing, "Rowe's story may reflect something which actually happened, although it if does, it seems unlikely to have been anything to do with the events now collectively known as the Roswell Incident...No reliable testimony has been given and no records have been found to support Rowe's account, and despite agreeing to do so, she has yet to sign an affidavit spelling out her story."

Once again, the facts as determined by others don't quite match those found by Pflock. First and foremost is that Rowe, and her sister Helen Cahill, have signed affidavits. Rowe gave them to me in March 1994 while I was in Roswell. She objected to the affidavit prepared by the Fund for UFO Research's Fred Whiting, nor did she appreciate the tactics of Pflock and others trying to get the affidavit signed.

Pflock looks at the story told by Rowe, pointing out, correctly, that she said her father had gone a fire run outside the city limits, arriving at the site where the crash had been discovered. Pflock said that he had spoken to three retired members of the fire department and one former city council member who said it was standing policy not to make runs outside the city limits. He writes, "...although Kevin Randle reports finding a record of another [fire run outside the city] in June 1947, the month before." He notes the names and positions of those telling him this.

The fact is, the fire department did make runs outside the city limits, though rarely. On June 21, at 10:50 P.M., the No. 4 pumper traveled 31 miles to fight some kind of fire.

Hector Trujillo, a current member of the Roswell Fire

Department said they travel into the county, north and west of the city to fight fires because there is no one else to do it. East and south of Roswell there are other fire departs handle the calls.

There are some other areas of corroboration for the Rowe story. She mentions the threats to her made by a "big Army man." The memories came flooding back when she heard the host of a radio talk show in Boston speaking. His New England accent triggered those memories for her.

Interestingly, in Pflock's report, he writes of an important new development. He tells about Glenn Dennis remembering something based on a blinding flash created as Don Schmitt outlined some of our new findings (labeled as revisionist by Pflock). Pflock writes, "He told me it was one of those unbidden, blinding flashes of recall which all of us sometimes have, bringing back to mind a bit of information which no amount of conscious effort had previously succeeded in calling up." Pflock accepts this sudden flash as legitimate, leading to specific conclusions outlined by him.

Frankie Rowe experienced the same kind of flash when the Boston radio show host spoke. Schmitt, who was in the room with her said that her face turned pure white and she was unable to speak. "It was one of those unbidden, blinding flashes of recall which all of us sometimes have, bringing to mind a bit of information."

Since Schmitt was there when it happened, he was able to observe her physical reaction to the sound of the man's voice. He saw how upset she had become. It was not a case of Frankie Rowe trying to convince anyone of the validity of her story, but a sincere reaction to the unexpected outside stimulus.

The question that comes to mind is why the double standard? Pflock accepts the testimony from Glenn

Dennis without asking critical questions. Yet, with Frankie Rowe, even with the corroboration of her sister and others, Pflock wonders if there is anything of value to her testimony.

The double standard is most evident when Pflock notes, "Rowe has appeared on "Good Morning America," has been interviewed for "48 Hours," and has appeared in the video tape, "UFO Secret: The Roswell Crash" (New Century Productions)." All true, but Pflock fails to note that Glenn Dennis appeared in or on all those shows and many others as well.

General Exon and More Corroboration

Pflock, in his report, dismisses the testimony of Brigadier General Arthur Exon, explaining that Exon never saw the bodies or the debris personally. Exon heard, from those he knew at the base that the bodies were coming there. He heard, from those he knew, that the debris was being tested there. The proper facilities for testing and exploiting the material were housed at the Wright Field Patterson Field complex that became Wright-Patterson AFB.

The Air Force investigators, though they knew what Exon had said, never bothered to interview him. His testimony could have seriously damaged their belief that Project Mogul was responsible for the debris found by Mac Brazel.

In fact, Exon told us during the interviews conducted with him, "We heard the material was coming to Wright Field...Everything from chemical analysis, stress tests, compression tests, flexing...I don't how it arrived but the boys who tested it said it was very unusual."

Exon said, "...some of it was flimsy and was tougher than hell and other almost like foil but strong. It had them pretty puzzled." Exon went farther, saying, "They knew they had something new in their hands. The metal and material was unknown to anyone I talked to...A couple of guys thought it might be Russian but the overall consensus was that the pieces were something from space."

Exon's testimony, admittedly second hand but from discussions he had with those who had first-hand knowledge and who were involved in the testing, suggests the debris is something more than the polyethylene balloons. The lab technicians at Wright Field should have been able to identify the components of a Mogul balloon array train even if they couldn't identify it specifically as coming from a Mogul balloon. Surely they wouldn't have told Exon that they "had something new in their hands."

But Exon did have some first-hand knowledge. He told Schmitt, "[It was] probably part of the same accident, but [there were] two distinct sites. One, assuming that the thing as I understand it, as I remember flying the area later, that the damage to the vehicle seemed to be coming from the southeast to the northwest, but it could have been going in the opposite direction, but that doesn't seem likely. So the farther northwest pieces were found on the ranch, those pieces were mostly metal."

What Exon has done, which badly damages the Mogul theory, is tie the two sites together. If what crashed was nothing more than the remains of a Mogul balloon, there wouldn't be "two distinct sites." In fact, there should be nothing left for Exon to see when he flew over those sites later. The debris would have been collected and the only way that Exon could see something is if the object that crashed had created a gouge on the ground.

Stanton Friedman entered the controversy, claiming to have called Exon to read him portions of *UFO Crash at Roswell*. According to Friedman, Exon told him that Schmitt and I had misquoted him. However, each of the quotes is on tape and each agrees exactly with what Exon said during the interviews conducted with him.

On November 24, 1991 I received a letter from Exon that clarified that situation. He stresses that he knew nothing first hand and that Schmitt and I, in our reporting, were responsible for the emphasis on his words. But he also acknowledges that he flew over the sites later, "much later."

The important point of this letter is his statement, "I remember auto tracks leading to the pivotal sites and obvious gouges in the terrain." Gouges that had been reported by others who were on the scene. Gouges that wouldn't have been made as the array train from a Mogul balloon returned to Earth. Gouges which Pflock and the Air Force never acknowledge nor explain and which, if true, tend to eliminate Mogul as the culprit in the Roswell case.

Which Way Was the Wind Blowing?

With no solid documentation about Flight No. 9's final resting place, Pflock's culprit for spreading debris, we are forced to guess. Pflock, based on the shaky testimony of three witnesses suggests that it fell on the Brazel ranch to be misidentified.

However, we do have documentation about both Flight No. 8 and Flight No. 10. Flight No. 8 was found down in the Tularosa valley northwest of Alamogordo. The terrain was too rough for them to recover the equipment, but they did find it. Flight No. 10 was last seen over Albuquerque, northwest of Alamogordo. There is no record of it being recovered.

Of course, with that data we can eliminate both those flights. The balloons were either seen on the ground or in the air in locations that would exclude them from landing on the Brazed ranch.

Using the Project Mogul documentation we learn a few other facts. First, Flight No. 8 was launched at 3:03 MST on July 3. The flight lasted 195 minutes (3 hours, 15 minutes) before it landed. The general track was to the northwest.

Just over forty-eight hours later, Flight No. 10 was launched at 5:01 MST. The flight lasted over 512 minutes (8 hours, 32 minutes) until it was lost over Albuquerque. The general track was to the northwest.

Between these two was Flight No. 9, launched about 1930 MST (7:30 PM) from Alamogordo. No data about the direction of flight or the location of its wreckage has been found to date. However, we know the direction taken by the balloon launched before it and the direction of the balloon launched after it. Both flew in a generally north*western* direction. It seems reasonable to assume, then, that Flight No. 9 flew in a similar direction, or to the northwest. The Brazel ranch is to the northeast of Alamogordo.

All the flights probably followed a more or less northerly course. Given that both Flight No. 8 and Flight No. 10 were found down or seen to the northwest of Alamogordo, it seems reasonable to assume that Flight No. 9 followed a similar path. Without precise winds aloft data, this is, of course, speculation, but it is reasonable speculation. From those two flights, there is no reason to assume that Flight No. 9 would have taken a different track, and there is no reason to assume that winds shifted from the northwesterly direction to a northeasterly direction and then back again. It certainly is possible, but not very likely.

What this means simply, is that the tracks of the balloons launched little more than twelve hours before Flight No. 9, and about 36 hours after it, gives us the ground track for the flights. It suggests that the balloon would not come within sixty miles of the Brazel ranch, and would be traveling away from it.

The Very End of Project Mogul

With the documentation available, the Air Force and Pflock reinvented the balloon. It wasn't a rawin target device as suggested by the Army, but, as the Air Force and Pflock would have us believe, a highly classified balloon belonging to Project Mogul. It is clear from the available testimony of those involved and from the documentation, that balloons were being launched in the right time frame in the right locations. By ignoring a large body of eyewitness testimony, by accepting as accurate the dubious statements of three civilians who were only marginally involved, Mogul could be suggested as a viable explanation.

In fact, according to Pflock, Charles Moore, one of the men deeply involved with Mogul said that there had been undocumented launches at some point. Moore also said that in the report prepared for New York University, some of the launches had been "classified out." In other words, they weren't in the report because they were highly classified.

The officers of Project Sign researched this problem for the Air Materiel Command in 1949. That report was originally classified at the same level as Project Mogul in 1949. They had access to all the data and learned Launch No. 8 was made on July 3 and Launch No. 10 on July 5. Both balloons and the attached array trains were located, neither anywhere near the the Brazel ranch, as we have seen.

Pflock, in his report writes, "It is all but certain that at least the great majority if not all of what was found at the debris field on the Foster Ranch was the wreckage of a huge balloon and instrumentation array launched from Alamogordo AAF as part of the 'crash' Top Secret, highly sensitive Project Mogul."

There is one other interesting point. By the acceptance of Mogul Launch No. 9, Pflock is accepting the scenario created by Schmitt and me, and information supplied by Frank Kaufmann. The conventional wisdom had always been for the crash on July 2. If that is a fact, then Mac Brazel couldn't have found the debris from Mogul Launch No. 9 because it hadn't yet been launched. Pflock finds himself in a dilemma. He must accept the "Revisionist History" because the dates don't work otherwise. Yet he rejects a great deal of the "revisionist" work because it doesn't fit his theory.

Dr. Charles Moore has also said that he doesn't believe that a Mogul balloon is responsible for the debris. What this means is that Moore doesn't believe it was one of the polyethylene balloons. He doesn't believe the July 3 launch caused the debris to be scattered. He does believe it was a balloon launched by the Mogul project, though one sent aloft early in June. So Moore disagrees with Pflock's conclusion.

The bottom line here is that there is no hard evidence for either the Air Force's or Pflock's Mogul theory. The documentation presented to date does not confirm it, and the testimony suggesting it is weak. Dr. Moore, in fact, said that it couldn't have been one of the polyethylene balloons. With that Mogul has been effectively eliminated as the culprit.

The front gate at the Roswell Industrial Park, at one time the main entrance to the Roswell Army Air Field.
Photo courtesy Kevin D. Randle

Overall Conclusions

The conclusions to be drawn seem evident. No persuasive evidence that what was found by Mac Brazel was anything other than a Project Mogul balloon has been offered. Instead, we are asked to reject a great deal of eyewitness testimony, not because it is flawed, but because it can't be crammed into the balloon theory framework. If we overlook that, if we assume that those reporting a craft and bodies are just looking for their fifteen minutes of fame, then a case for Mogul might be possible.

The Air Force settled on Mogul Launch No. 4, which was so unimportant that they didn't log it in their official reports, it was not in the NYU information reviewed, and didn't appear in any other documentation except a personal diary. That report tells us that the balloons were nothing more spectacular than normal meteorological balloons. There may have been rawin targets on it, there might have been other equipment attached to it, but the records only show that it carried a sonobuoy. We can argue that it carried nothing other than the sonobuoy so that there was no metallic debris to be found by Mac Brazel. It might have come down on the Brazel ranch, but then it might not. There is no documentation to support a crash on the Brazel ranch. Launch No. 4 was so unimportant that the Mogul staff didn't try to find it, though with later launches they did chase the balloons.

The Air Force investigators said they found no persua-

An investigator uses a metal detector on the debris field searching for any signs of remains of the object that crashed. Several such searches have failed to produce results.

Photo courtesy Kevin D. Randle

sive evidence that anyone was sworn to secrecy and in fact, print the statement from Sheridan Cavitt that he was not. However Major (later Colonel) Edwin Easley, when first contacted about the flying saucer crash in July 1947 said, "I can't talk about it. I was sworn to secrecy." The Air Force never asked about these statements never challenged me about them. They just ignored them.

When all the evidence is examined, we learn that there were more than just the three witnesses (Brazel, Marcel and Cavitt) to debris on the Brazel ranch the Air Force names, and we learn there was more than one crash site. We learn there are named witnesses to the craft and bodies, and we learn from Air Force Brigadier General Arthur Exon that he flew over both sites sometime later. All these facts are ignored by Air Force investigators because they are the "verbal reports many years after the alleged incident occurred."

The Air Force, in the conclusion of their report, provided a number of reasons why there had been no mention of "alien bodies" by them. Those conclusions are ludicrous on the surface. To further reject the idea because there is disagreement among the various UFO groups and researchers is also ridiculous. All of us agree that there was a crash in New Mexico, that there were bodies recovered from that crash, and that those bodies were taken out of the state by government and military officials. While the precise details might be in dispute, the basic and important facts are not.

Further, to suggest that the claims of those who saw the bodies "are often attributed to people using pseudonyms," is, at best, misleading. In my work I used one pseudonym because the witness feared, not retribution by the government, but UFO researchers demanding that he tell them the story too. When the name of a witness becomes known to the general public, there are those who want to verify it themselves. That attitude is completely understandable. I often feel the same way. I want to make sure that the reporter is telling all the facts so that I can make an intelligent decision about the validity of a case. However, that doesn't mean the witness is lying or that the facts aren't as reported.

Finally, to suggest that those making the biggest claims about alien bodies make their living from the "Roswell Incident" is a gross misrepresentation. I do not make my living off Roswell. With Don Schmitt, I have, on the other hand, interviewed more than 500 people during more than two thousand interviews in our attempt to learn the truth. We have interviewed everyone of the witnesses to whom the Air Force spoke with the exception of Dr. Spilhaus. We had no agenda when we began. Can the Air Force investigators make a similar claim?

The Air Force has now tried the same explanation they used forty years ago. It is amazing that anyone would listen to it, especially when it is remembered they didn't interview very many of the witnesses. They set out to prove an answer and satisfied themselves. That isn't investigation, it isn't science, but it is propaganda.

Of course, they do have support for their belief. Karl Pflock agreed that the debris was a Project Mogul balloon array train, he just selected a different flight. Instead of Flight No. 4, Pflock selected No. 9. There are problems with it too, but different ones.

Pflock offered three witnesses to corroborate his point of view, Bessie Brazel Schrieber, Jason Kellahin, and "Reluctant." Bessie Brazel's testimony is contradicted by her brother Bill, the Proctors, Stricklands, and Sultemeiers. We must believe that she could identify materials found as a balloon but Major Jesse Marcel, among many other military and civilian authorities, could not. Jason Kellahin's testimony is contradicted by Robin Adair, the documented evidence, and by his own testimony in his first interviews with Dr. Mark Rodeghier, Don Schmitt, and me. Reluctant's story is contradicted by his own earlier statements and by his claim to have samples of the debris. He could prove his case easily if he could find the debris and submit it for analysis.

Those who saw the debris and describe it as extremely unusual include Jesse Marcel, Sr., Jesse Marcel, Jr., Frank Kaufmann, Lewis Rickett, Robert Smith, Ellis Boldra, Bill Brazel, Jim Ragsdale, Frankie Rowe, Sallye Tadolini, and on and on.

Each of these witnesses said that the material was like nothing they had ever seen. While they might not have seen polyethylene before this event, there is nothing that extraordinary about polyethylene. It looks like rubberized plastic but isn't. It can be folded but does not unfold itself without a sign of a crease. The witnesses also describe light weight material, as thin as newsprint that can't be dented or bent. The question that comes to mind is if this was part of the Mogul array train, where is that material today? It just hasn't been presented.

For either of the Mogul theories to work, we must throw out a great deal of eyewitness testimony because it doesn't fit into the Mogul construct. We must accept the shaky testimony of three people and eliminate the eyewitness testimony of almost four dozen others. No good reasons have been presented for eliminating all that testimony.

Much of the testimony has been eliminated only by suggesting that the Mac Brazel find was a Mogul Balloon, but the impact site might have been something more. Pflock attempts to suggest two events and two separate sites, overlooking the testimony of Brigadier General Arthur Exon and Robin Adair that tie those two sites together. When that is remembered, and that there are nearly a dozen first-hand witnesses to the craft and bodies including Major Edwin Easley, Dr. W. Curry Holden, and Lewis Rickett, it becomes clear that Mogul fails to explain the evidence.

Both the Air Force investigators and Pflock have settled on Mogul as the answer to the Roswell case. They present some testimony that when examined on the surface makes a great case for Project Mogul as the culprit. However, when all the evidence is examined, the evidence for Mogul fails.

All alternative explanations offered to date, when examined, fail on one point. They cannot account for all the testimony. To make any explanation work, regardless of what it is, eyewitness testimony must be eliminated. Project Mogul does not explain the debris found, the gouge in the terrain, or the different types of material. It does not explain the eyewitness testimony of a craft and bodies. And if the theory cannot explain all the evidence, then the theory must be flawed.

In the course of the investigation, I have examined a large number of theories. For a period there were explanations that were accepted as reliable only to be rejected later. Some thought it was a Japanese balloon bomb, an experimental aircraft, a Skyhook balloon, a regular aircraft accident that involved classified material, a Flying Wing, a V-2 rocket, a V-2 rocket carrying midgets, or children, or even ex-Nazis. Each has been examined carefully and rejected. Even the Air Force agreed that none of these other theories fit the facts. They reduced it to a single launch and then provided no documentation for it. Pflock reduced it to a different launch and provided no documentation for it.

That documentation has been found and reviewed. Nothing in it suggests that Mogul was responsible. Yes, there was a launch on June 4, 1947 but they don't know what happened to those balloons and equipment. Yes, the balloons of Flight No. 9 were launched, but the mission itself was scrubbed. There was no special equipment and no evidence of what happened to the balloons.

For the Mogul explanation to be proved, someone is going to have to find documents that place the balloons down on the Brazel ranch. Someone is going to have to present something more solid than idle speculations, regardless of the backgrounds of those being quoted. The debris described with Mogul resembles that found by Brazel and others in a very gross sense but it doesn't match.

Project Mogul has done nothing to explain the Roswell case. It has muddied the waters and provided those who don't want to believe with a ready made answer. It wasn't a spaceship, it was a balloon.

But those who were there, those who saw the debris, saw the craft, and saw the bodies, the truth is self-evident. The object that crashed at Roswell was designed, constructed and first flown on another planet. Of that, there can be no doubt.

Don Schmitt stands among the brush and trees at the base of the cliff where the craft crashed.

Photo courtesy Kevin D. Randle

Interviews Conducted with Various Witnesses

The search for the truth at Roswell has been a long and difficult one. Don Schmitt and I have conducted more than two thousand interviews with more than five hundred people. To put together this work, not all that data was used. The following is a list of the major, relevant witnesses used here. It does not reflect all the work done, all the witnesses interviewed, but does provide the source data.

1. Robin Adair Associated Press reporter was interviewed by Don Schmitt in December 1992 on audio tape. Interviewed by telephone in January 1993, handwritten notes.

2, Dr. George Agogino was interviewed by Tom Carey a number of times. Audio taped interview was conducted on August 1, 1993.

3. Ruben Anaya> was interviewed by Don Schmitt, handwritten notes. Video tape interview conducted November 15, 1991. Brother Pete and his wife Mary interviewed on February 2, 1992 and corroborate the story.

4. Bill Brazed, Jr.# was interviewed on February 23, 1989, audio-taped. Additional interviews were conducted in March 1989, September 1990, July 1992 and December 1992. Several of these were audio taped.

5. Sheridan Cavitt was interviewed on January 29,

Standing at the base of the cliff and looking back, toward the northwest where the craft crashed.

Photo courtesy Kevin D. Randle

1990 in Sierra Vista, Arizona and in March 1993 and on June 25, 1994, handwritten notes. Telephone interview conducted on August 8, 1989 with notes.

6. Glenn Dennis[#], the Roswell mortician in 1947 was videotaped on November 19, 1990 by Mark Wolf, November 22, 1990 video-taped, May 30, 1994 audio taped, as well as various personal interviews with hand-written notes. David Wagnon, interviewed in July 1994 corroborates the existence of the nurse that Dennis has mentioned as part of his report. Former Roswell chief of police, E.M. Hall has also corroborated a portion of Dennis' story.

7. Brigadier General Thomas J. DuBose, video-taped in August 1990, video tape supplied to FUFOR. Various telephone conversations conducted by Don Schmitt and letter from DuBose about the events in General Ramey's office.

8. Barbara Dugger, granddaughter of Sheriff George Wilcox was video-taped in March 1992 and a copy of the tape was supplied to FUFOR.

9. Major (later Colonel) Edwin Easley[*+**] was interviewed January 11, 1990 audio-taped and supplied to Fund for UFO Research (FUFOR), February 2, 1990 handwritten notes, June 23, 1990, audio taped, August 13, 1990, audio taped...after that point Easley was too sick to be interviewed. Some information about crash supplied by daughters Nancy Strickland and Shelly Perkins (to Randle and Schmitt), and his physician Dr. Harold Granik (to Rodeghier April 14, 1992).

10. Brigadier General Arthur Exon was interviewed on May 19, 1990, audio taped, June 18, 1990, audio taped with handwritten notes, at Wright-Patterson AFB, July 1990, and provided written confirmation of accuracy of quotes used on November 24, 1991.

11. Thomas Gonzales[*+] interviewed first by John Price, UFO Enigma Museum and Don Ecker, UFO videotaped,

and on July 19, 1994 audio taped.

12. Walter Haut was interviewed on April 1, 1989, audio taped, April 20, 1989, audio-taped.

13. Sappho Henderson was interviewed on January 21, 1990, audio taped, August 20, 1991, video tape supplied to FUFOR. Other videotaped statements made to *Unsolved Mysteries,* August 1989.

14. Dr. W. Curry Holden[*+**] was interviewed in person November 21, 1993, hand-written notes. Daughter J. Kelly was interviewed by Mark Rodeghier in 1990 and on audio tape on December 5, 1992. Holden died before a follow-up interview could be arranged.

15. Frank Joyce, interviewed on March 30, 31, 1989, videotaped interview March 1991. Copy of the video tape supplied to FUFOR.

16. Frank Kaufmann[*+#] was interviewed a number of times, including video-taped on September 28, 1990, audio tape March 25, 1993 and April 24, 1993, videotaped March 27, 1994. Notes were taken at various other meetings including June 28, 1993. Kaufmann has also been interviewed by Kent Jeffrey, Col. Jeff Jeffrey, Mark Rodeghier and Phil Jones of CBS News.

17. Jason Kellahin was interviewed by Dr. Mark Rodeghier on November 24, 1992, handwritten notes, audio taped interview conducted in November 1992, videotaped interview conducted on January 28, 1993.

18. Jesse Marcel, Sr.[#] was interviewed by Bob Pratt, December 1979, audio-taped. Other taped interviews include those broadcast on In Search Of... in 1980 and on WWL-TV in New Orleans conducted by John Mann. Linda Corley conducted the first recorded interview with Marcel in 1970.

19. Jesse Marcel, Jr.[#] interviewed conducted in August 1989, notes, May 1990, video-taped and July 1990, videotaped and August 18, 1990 audio taped. Other interviews

were conducted by telephone in November 1989, January 1990 and April 1990.

20. John McBoyle[*+>] of KSWS in Roswell was interviewed December 5, 1990, hand-written notes.

21. Phyllis McGuire was interviewed in January 1990, handwritten notes, video tape interview in November 1990. Fred Whiting of FUFOR videotaped an interview with McGuire in July 1990.

22. Art McQuiddy was[>] interviewed on January 19, 1990 on audio tape.

23. Charles B. Moore was interviewed on September 6, 1994 and September 10, 1994, hand-written notes.

24. Irving Newton interviewed on March 1, 1990, audio taped and December 1991, audio taped.

25. Loretta Proctor[#] was interviewed on April 20, 1989, audio-taped, July 1990 videotaped by FUFOR, and in November 1990, videotaped by Randle.

26. Norris Proctor was interviewed in March 1990 about his mother and brother's involvement in the case, audio taped.

27. Robert Porter, interviewed by Don Schmitt, May 1991, conducted by Don Schmitt, audio taped.

28. Corporal E.L. Pyles[<] was interviewed by Don Schmitt in December 1993.

29. Jim Ragsdale[*+#] was Interviewed 26 Jan 1993 audio-taped, affidavit signed January 27, 1993, April 24 written notes, August 1993 verbal. Various family members were in attendance, including his wife and his son, and have corroborated his telling of the story for decades, as noted at the bottom of the book page...Mark Rodeghier has heard confirmation from family members.

30. LaTone Ramey, wife of Lieutenant General Roger M. Ramey, hand-written notes on March 25, 1991. She married Ramey after the events of 1947 and said she knew nothing about it.

31. Lewis Rickett[+#**] was interviewed by phone May 1989, Nov 1989, Dec 1989, Jan 1990, Feb 1990, Mar 1990, audio taped interviews Jan 1990 by Mark Rodeghier (about two hours), videotaped Aug 1990 (supplied to FUFOR). Final interviewed was conducted by Don Schmitt just two weeks prior to Rickett's death. Hand-written notes.

32. George "Jud" Roberts[**>], minority owner of KGFL was interviewed January 19, 1990, audio taped, January 31, 1990, audio taped, and videotaped September 27, 1990, tape supplied to FUFOR. Lydia Sleppy reported her teletype transmission from radio station KSWS was interrupted by the FBI providing one level of corroboration for Roberts. She was interviewed on February 5, 1993, audio taped.

33. Frankie Rowe[#>] has been interviewed a number of times, including a video-taped interview January 1993 supplied to FUFOR and audio taped interviews October 3, 1990. Rowe has provided video-taped statements to reporters for *48 Hours,* and *Good Morning America.* Frankie's sister, Helen Cahill corroborates part of her story, interview conducted in September 1993, handwritten notes.

34. Don Schmitt interviewed a flight crew member who was on one of the flights that took a huge crate from Roswell in June 1989, handwritten notes.

35. Dr. C. Bertrand Schultz[**] was interviewed a number of times by Tom Carey, video-taped interview (conducted by Randle) April 25, 1993, both daughters, Donna Wilcox and Tranda Schultz, have confirmed his telling the story for decades, as has Dr. W.D. Frankforter.

36. Robert Slusher, videotaped interview conducted on March 3, 1991. Other interviews were conducted by telephone, handwritten notes.

37. Robert Smith[#], interviewed audio-taped on Janu-

ary 8, 1990. Additional information provided by letter, January 21, 1990. Videotaped interview conducted on March 2, 1990 and copy supplied to FUFOR.

38. Leo Spear was interviewed in May 1993, handwritten notes, audio taped interview conducted on June 3, 1993.

39. Marian Strickland was interviewed on January 4, 1990, audio taped, September 27, 1990 videotaped and supplied to FUFOR. Both Easley and Colonel Joe Briley (Operations Officer of the 509th, interviewed October 20, 1989) have corroborated part of her story about Brazed.

40. Len Stringfield's source, known as Tim, was interviewed by Don Schmitt twice, handwritten notes. Stringfield has also shared some of his data about Tim with me.

41. Sallye Tadolini interviewed on December 1, 1991, audio taped.

42. Colonel A. C. Trakowski was interviewed on September 7, 1994.

43. Elizabeth Tulk was interviewed in January 1990, handwritten notes. Videotaped in July 1990 by Fred Whiting at FUFOR.

44. George Walsh was interviewed on March 24, 1990 on audio tape.

45. Donna Wilcox was interviewed on May 19, 1993, audio taped. He sister Tranda has also been interviewed by Tom Carey and corroborates her story.

46. William Woody[**<] was interviewed September 30, 1990 handwritten notes, November 21, 1990 video-taped, May 1, 1994 by Mark Rodeghier and Kent Jeffrey, handwritten notes.

47. Walt Whitmore,[#] Jr. was interviewed in September 1990, handwritten notes.

*Eyewitnesses to the recovery of alien bodies.
+Eyewitnesses to the craft.

#Either saw or handled debris from the debris field or the impact site.

**Eyewitness to the military cordon.

<Eyewitness to the object in the sky.

>Eyewitness to threats by governmental officials.

Col. William Blanchard, Commanding Officer of the 509th Bomb Group in July, 1947.

Photo courtesy Kevin D. Randle

Part II: Transcripts and Affidavits from Witness Interviews

1. Brigadier General Arthur Exon—June 18, 1990. He talks of two distinct sites and flying over those sites himself.

2. Letter from Brigadier General Exon confirming that the quotes in the book *UFO Crash at Roswell* were accurate.

3. Colonel Joe Briley—October 20, 1989. He confirms that Col. Blanchard's leave was a blind so that Blanchard could work the impact site with questions from the media about where he was.

4. Major (later Colonel) Edwin Easley—January 11, 1990. Easley confirms that he was sworn to secrecy about the events of July 1947.

5. Loretta Proctor—April 20, 1989. Descriptions of the debris found by Mac Brazel as shown to her and why that debris is inconsistent with that from a Project Mogul Balloon.

7. George "Jud" Roberts—January 19, 1990. Roberts confirms that the license of radio station KGFL was threatened and that military officials cordoned the area.

8. Affidavit from Helen Cahill—Daughter of Roswell fire fighter Dan Dwyer.

10. Affidavit from Brigadier General Thomas J.

The Atomic Blast

O-DAY IS CELEBRATED

VIP's Present On O-Day

OPERATIONAL DAY

BIKINI

NAGASAKI

HIROSHIMA

Personalities

Formations

R. A. A. F.

SOUVENIR ISSUE

The Atomic Blast showing the staff of the 509th in July, 1947.

Photo courtesy Kevin D. Randle

DuBose—Chief of Staff, Eighth Air Force Headquarters, July 1947.

11. Affidavit from Barbara Dugger—Granddaughter of Sheriff George Wilcox.

12. Affidavit from First Lieutenant Walter Haut—Public Relations Officer, 509th Bomb Group, July 1947.

13. Affidavit from Dr. John Kronschroeder—Handled the metallic debris.

14. Affidavit from Jim Ragsdale—Saw the craft and bodies on the impact site and handled the metallic debris.

15. Affidavit from George "Jud" Roberts—Minority owner of radio station KGFL in July 1947.

16. Affidavit from Frankie Rowe—Daughter of fire fighter Dan Dwyer, handled debris and was threatened by a military officer in July 1947.

17. Affidavit from Sergeant Robert Smith—Loaded cargo for 1st Air Transport Unit station at Roswell in July 1947 and handled a piece of metallic debris.

18. Affidavit of William Woody—Saw the object come down and saw the military cordon.

Phyllis McGuire, daughter of Sherif George Wilcox, was a witness to the events in the Sheriff's Office.
Photo courtesy Paul Davids

Arthur E. Exon, Brigadier General, Wright-Patterson AFB June 18, 1990

They discuss who Hynek was, what the Center was, and what Don's interest in the subject was. Don mentions that he follows the military cases and that it's like a black hole. Much goes in but nothing comes out.

AEE: I'm not surprised at that because like your predecessors in this business, the people that were most intimate with this thing years ago died. And with them went a lot of information. I don't know what records were kept, or what files were kept. And sometimes I think that maybe was the reason why everything has been so quiet. People die and everybody kept quiet until most of the thirteen or so who were involved and their staff people had passed on.

DRS: It's a self perpetuating cover up. Information is lost in time.

AEE: Yeah, and most of the people you're talking to are a little bit like me. Close enough to know there was something happening. They had no direct responsibility for any of it. It was classified. And so, even the people who might have worked for the staff of thirteen that started it

Jay and Elizabeth Tulk. Both were in the Sheriff's Office during the critical period in July, 1947.
Photo courtesy Paul Davids

off, had people there who were right in handling all this stuff but they were near to it. They got all the information.

DRS: Talks to him about being a POW. Exon says it was a year and nine days. Down in April, 1944 and liberated in April, 1945. In North Africa and then in Italy. Talks about his moving from camp to camp. Was a Major. When Russians broke through, moved by train, walking...then Americans broke through, moved again. Was along year. Talks about the Battle of Bulge. Rather have the action. Sensed the end of the war. Knew it was coming. Knew things were moving fast. Never as fast as a POW wanted.

AEE:...investigate a UFO. Well, we would make an airplane available, scheduled, things like that.

DRS: What type of airplane?

AEE: Usually at that time they were T-39s, twin jets, and lots of times we sent a 240, Convair 240 with a crew and they would go and these guys would do their business and they'd sit an air base someplace and cool it until the guys came back. They'd come back, drop them off and go about their business.

DRS: How big a team was it?

AEE: I can't remember. Sometimes it would be eight and sometimes it would be fifteen. And most of the people...

DRS: They were assigned to Wright-Pat?

AEE: No. They were, they would come from Washington, D.C. And they'd ask for an airplane tomorrow morning and that would give the guys a chance to get there by commercial airline, to meet them. The airplane would take off at such and such a time. Sometimes they'd be gone for three days and sometimes they'd be gone for a week. I know they went out to Montana and Wyoming and the northwest states a number of times in a year and a half that I recall. There probably were other places. They went to Arizona once or twice.

DRS: Was there any name for the operation?

AEE: Well, I...no, I don't recall that there was. Our contact was a man, a telephone number. He'd call and he's set the airplane up. I just knew there was an investigative team. There probably was a name but I...

...Stuart Symington, who was Secretary of Defense, Carl Spaatz...all these guys at the top of government. They were the ones who knew the most about Roswell, New Mexico. They were involved in what to do about the residue from that...those two findings.

DRS: You say those two.

AEE: Probably part of the same accident but two distinct sites. One, assuming that the thing, as I understand it, as I remember flying the area later, that the damage to the vehicle seemed to be coming from southeast to northwest but it could have been going in the opposite direction but it doesn't seem likely. So the farther northwest pieces found on the ranch, those pieces were mostly metal...

...couldn't be easily ripped or changed...you could change it. You could wad it up you could change the shape but it was still there and ...there were other parts of it that were very thin but awfully strong and couldn't be dented with heavy hammers and stuff like that...which at that time were causing some people some concern...again, say it was a shape of some kind you could grab this end and bend it but it would come right back. It was flexible to a degree.

DRS: What type of testing would they have been capable at the lab?

AEE: I think the full range of testing was possible. Everything from chemical analysis, and resist chemicals, stress tests, compression tests, flexing, all this kind of stuff. They would probably be able to match it with things they knew. I don't know, at that time, if was titanium or some other metal that...or if it was something they knew about and the processing was something different...

DRS: Do you recall if the atmosphere or the whole attitude at the base was different at that time?

AEE: No...It was a long time after 1947...I believe, it was, I was in the Pentagon. I was there five and a half years from 55 to 60. That was the time period that we lost the four airplanes down there (Kentucky, Tennessee). And during that period some time, I can't remember just how it came up but I Forrestal, Truman, Spaatz, Symington, I'm sure there were more guys next to Spaatz, like intelligence guys or some information type close to him at the Pentagon and to Forrestal, CIA, and I know it was just more than military. I can't remember how this came about exactly but I...I'm trying to put a time period with this because I can't figure out for sure why I had any reason to come up on that subject unless it was just the fact we were investigating, that the Air Force was trying to find those airplanes down in Kentucky and this came up.

In there some place, and maybe it was the command post guy or somebody in operations...in a confidential meeting was telling them about Blue Book and ah, there were supposed to be thirteen, as I remember it, thirteen that were named in that outfit and were sworn to secrecy. And they were those fellows I mentioned or people who were damned closed to them.

In the '55 time period, there was also the story that whatever happened, whatever was found at Roswell was still a closely held and probably would be held until these fellows I mentioned had died so they wouldn't be embarrassed or they wouldn't have to explain why they covered it up.

...if they needed to bring in other specialists, they did.

...if a guy came on he knew that he was working on a project that was Department of Defense business and he was to protect it. So back to that original thirteen, I think ...until the original thirteen die off and I don't think anyone is going to release anything the last one's gone.

DRS: We still have witnesses involved with Roswell that tell us they are sworn to secrecy or at least that's still their perception...they will go to their graves honoring their commitments.

AEE: I'd do the same thing. You'd just be hazed and hassled by everybody who was trying to reconstruct the thing and the guy after 50 years plus...

I don't want anything to happen here that is not good. When I say good, I mean that would weaken the security of the country and the public attitude toward their government. If the government covered up at that time the nature of things...we had sputnik and people were shaky enough, that, releasing the information would cause a clamor for information that the government couldn't provide because they didn't know. And we're still investigating...they're investigating to this day.

24 Nov '91

Kevin D. Randle

Cedar Rapids, Ia 52402

Dear Kevin

I'm sorry that a portion of my interview has given you trouble. I will acknowledge that the quote does have me saying that my flights later (much later) verified the direction of possible flight of the object. I remember auto tracks leading to pivotal sites and obvious gouges in terrain.

Further, you both likely recall on many occasions during my visits with you in person and on the phone when you wanted me to meet others — that I did not know anything first Hand. Although I believe you did quote me accurately, I do believe that in your Writings you gave more credence and impression of personal + direct knowledge than my recordings would indicate on their own! I felt that throughout the portions where my name was used, the quotes were O.K. but authoritative emphasis was yours. I want to say that so far your use of my name and discussions have not given me any problem. So lets leave it at that. I did enjoy your and Donalds efforts in digging into who knows what!

I'm returning the copy of you book. I'll be glad to pay for it but would appreciate it being autographed.

Best wishes.

Sincerely.

[illegible]

P.S. This was to be a draft — then typed but the ribbon has seen its best!

Sorry

[illegible]

Briley, Joe, Lt. Col. 509th Operations Officer, Transcript October 20, 1989

...first few moments of the tape are garbled and then have Bribed saying...And I had no idea that this was anything other than what they said. General Roger Ramey, the Eighth Air Force commander and he made a statement to the press that these young, eager commander was a little over enthused when he made his initial report on the spaceship landing. And that's all I know about it. I was a squadron commander ... I certainly was let in on this. And I heard no more about it.

KDR: I've got...you eventually became the S-3 I guess. I've got a copy of the yearbook that was produced in November, so you became the S-3 but at the time this happened...

JCH: I was probably the S-3 then. I got there in '46 and stayed until '48. I believe that I was just a squadron commander at the time.

KDR: Which annoys me no end but only because I'm trying to locate some of the staff members who would have attended the meeting on July 8, which is the day after Jesse Marcel calve back from the ranch with the material.

JCB: Well, I wasn't included in that.

KDR: But you know that Colonel Blanchard went to the site. (This is based on a statement he made earlier in the interview. I wanted to make sure that I had him on tape saying it.)

JCB: Yes. But he's dead now.

KDR: So is Jesse Marcel as a matter of tact. I son a number of times

JCB: Hopkins, I believe, was the S-3 then. He's dead too.

KDR: So you took over for, would it have been Colonel Hopkins?

JCB: He and I exchanged jobs sometime after that. He took my squadron and I took the S-3.

KDR: Do you know of anybody on the staff other than Major Saunders, whom I've also talked to, who night still be around?

JCB: No, I certainly don't. Not anyone who is still alive.

KDR: Did you know Major Izadore Brown very well?

JCB: Vaguely.

KDR: But you don't know what happened to him?

JCB: No .

KDR: You were on the base at the time. You heard stories...

JCB: Right. And then the story was changed and hushed up immediately. As soon as the people from Washington arrived.

KDR: As soon as the people from Washington arrived.

JCB: Right.

KDR: Do you know, by any chance, who might have been on that flight?

JCB: I have no idea at all. I just wasn't brought into that at all even though Butch (Blanchard) and I were extremely close friends. He was my instructor in flying school and we were very close...when this thing clamped the lid on, that was it. I'm sorry that I can't tell you any more than that. As a matter of fact I was real surprised when T heard this additional stuff about it.

KDR: You didn't have an opportunity to see the material...?

JCE: Not a thing. I didn't even take...it became such a...kind of a hoax deal that we all forgot it immediately.

KDR: What's your feeling about it now?

JCB: Well, I think they probably...that there's some truth to it because, in retrospect, I don't think Butch was stupid enough to call a weather balloon something else.

KDR: I've talked to a number of the staff officers at Roswell and I don't think any of them were stupid enough to fall for that. They'd have to be pretty inept...

JCB: Yeah. That's right. Course the way the thing was turned around it was a what-if thing before they actually got to the bottom of it. Conjecture and all. Frankly it was just hushed up so quickly that and so completely that nothing was ever said about it. Old Butch, over a few martinis, he'd let me in on a lot of family secrets and a lot of other stuff but I never heard anything about that.

KDR: Do you know if his first wife is still alive?

JCB: Ethyl? I'm sure she is.

KDR: Would you happen to know where she might be?

JCB: I have no idea. The last I heard, she was married to a doctor in Fort Worth.

KDR: You wouldn't happen to know his name?

JCB: I have no idea.

KDR: I found Ann Blanchard but unfortunately she doesn't know anything.

JCB: I don't think Ethyl would either. At that time they were on pretty thin ice. I'm sure that he didn't confide in her.

KDR: Did he have a daily type staff meeting?

JCB: I'm sure that he had his immediate staff around him most of the time but scheduled staff meetings I think he probably had one a week. I'm sure that he was in contact with his principals daily. As for Marcel was at the site, I don't know but I don't think anyone else went out there.

KDR: We know that Marcel when out there. Do you remember a man named Cavitt?

JCB: No, I don't believe I do.

KDR: How about Lewis Rickett?

JCB: No. I hate to sound so vague about this but I swear to God that I don't know much about it.

KDR: The thing is that it happened forty-two years ago.

JCB: No, the thing is that it just didn't circulate. We were in the A-bomb business. We all, as a matter of fact, I was among the second bunch of bomb commanders that were trained at Sandia. I was privy to a lot of information along that line. But on this particular thing I was completely shut out.

KDR: So you have no first hand knowledge?

JCB: Nothing at all.

KDR: You heard some stories around the base.

JCB: That first thing that was put out in the paper.

KDR: That you'd captured a flying saucer.

JCB: Yeah. Well, no, they'd found a crashed flying saucer.

KDR: It says, I believe, RAAF captures flying saucer.

JCB: Well, Whatever. Then, you've probably got this thing of Roger Ramey's that refuted the whole thing and said that his over-ambitious or, I don't remember how he said it...made Butch sound like a first grader, which I didn't buy but I didn't know any of the particulars.

KDR: Do you happen to know who the weather officer would been at the base at the time?

JCB: We a captain weather officer that was working with our navigators. At that time, they were doing what was called pressure pattern flying, single heading flight planning because of the rotation around highs and lows that taking off from a given point and knowing the atmospheric pressure you set a correction in your flight plan and by flying one magnetic heading you would wind up at your destination quicker than you would by flying in and out of the wind. (He goes into a long explanation of what all this entails which has nothing to do with the story.)

KDR: Would he have been the group weather officer?

JCB: Yes, he would have been.

KDR: The reason I'm pushing on this is the weather officer at Eighth Air Force which was a fellow named Irving Newton was brought in to identify the weather balloon and if I could find the weather officer from Roswell...

JCB: I don't think he would have been there.

KDR: But we could have contrasted here's a man who should have been able to identify it as well and was not able to do so.

JCB: I do know that there was a captain and he was a brilliant boy and he was working with this navigator that reduced all of the volume of computations into a graph.

KDR: Was the weather officer also a navigator?

JCB: No, I don't believe so. You talk about the Eighth Air Force man being a warrant officer. That was unusual because we always had commissioned officers as weather officers. I really can't remember any more than that and I'm sorry to take up your time.

KDR: That's fine.

JCB: This is very interesting to me. Actually getting like most of the citizens now and a cover-up don't surprise me.

KDR: I think we've pretty well established that. I've

looked at this stuff and I can't believe that Major Marcel and Colonel Blanchard and a number of other people at the 509th were so inept that they couldn't identify a weather balloon when shown bits and pieces of one.

JCB: I'm sure of that too.

KDR: But you have no first hand knowledge. Do you remember what it was like at the base in those first few days? Do you remember hearing the rumors? Do you remember anything like that?

JCB: When we read the local paper the day that this happened there was a big flap and then this was all discounted and I think was even turned into a hoax that some reporter had stretched it way beyond the truth. And then it was hushed up real well.

KDR: It was brilliantly hushed up. If Major Marcel hadn't had said something in 1978 we probably still wouldn't know about it.

JCB: I didn't know anything in '46 or '48 either or in '47.

KDR: So you were just the squadron commander in that time frame?

JCB: I'm sure of that.

KDR: So you wouldn't have been brought in no matter what happened.

JCB: That's right. Well, I don't think anyone in our group would. There's just a few who actually saw it. And naturally they wouldn't have gotten a bunch of people together to go out and look at it. I don't why Butch was sent out there or why he went out there except he was West Point and our group commander and he was pretty much into everything.

KDR: He was the group commander so he would have gone out in the beginning anyway, I suppose.

JCB: Not necessarily. If it had been just a weather balloon I don't think that would have justified him going out there.

KDR: But you know he went out there for a fact.

JCB: I'm sure of it.

KDR: And you don't remember much about this Washington team that came in.

JCB: I have no idea at all. If they landed on the base it was hush-hush. I heard nothing and I saw nothing.

KDR: And the next day you read the *Roswell Daily Record* and they said it was a weather balloon.

JCB: No. I...The first one was with the little men and all that business. That was the one they said was all a bunch of hoax but it was never, to my knowledge the local paper never retracted their story.

We then discuss Brazel a little bit and what might have happened there. We finally sign off with Briley agreeing to answer any other questions I might have.

Easley, Edwin D. Major, 509th Provost Marshall, Transcript January 11, 1990

KDR: I doing some research into the 509th Bomb Group and I understand that you were the Provost Marshal there at one time.

EDE: That's right.

KDR: At the 509th?

EDE: Yes.

KDR: During July of 1947?

EDE: Yes.

KDR: Pardon me.

EDE: Yes.

KDR: You're aware of the incident that took place there in July of 1947? The alleged crash of a flying saucer.

EDE: (long pause) I've heard about it.

KDR: Do you have any first hand knowledge of it?

EDE: I can't talk about it.

KDR: Then you do have some first hand knowledge?

EDE: I can't talk about it.

KDR: Ah-ha.

EDE: Ah-ha.

KDR: We have received information from a couple of

people that you had been out to the crash site yourself as the Provost Marshal. That is what we're trying to confirm. But you can't talk about it.

EDE: That's right.

KDR: Is there anything at all that you could tell me that might help me?

EDE: Help you what?

KDR: Help me learn exactly what happened there in July of 1947.

EDE: Well you should start with the former commander who was Colonel Blanchard but I believe that he has passed away.

KDR: Yes, he died in the...from a heart attack at the Pentagon.

EDE: Uh-huh.

KDR: I've talked to Colonel Briley who was the Operations Officer and Patrick Saunders who was the Base Adjutant and we've been in contact with...

EDE: Did you talk to the Intelligence Officer?

KDR: Jesse Marcel has talked...told us, told others what happened. We have some taped interviews with him telling what he had seen the days he was there. And we've talked to some of the other fellows Who were involved in the counter-intelligence end of it.

EDE: I would think they could tell you everything that you need to know.

KDR: Can you tell me if you were at the crash site?

EDE: I can't talk about it. I told you that.

KDR: Yes, sir, I understand that.

EDE: I've been sworn to secrecy. I can't tell you that.

KDR: Uh-huh.

EDE: I'm not going to talk about it.

KDR: Let me pose a hypothetical question that might help us here a little bit. Is there way...

EDE: Did you talk to the man who owned the land?

KDR: Yes,

EDE: He ought to be able to tell you a lot more...

KDR: I've talked to the Brazel family and to the people who are the current residents. I've talked to Walter Haut. I talked to an awful lot of people...The question I want to ask and I want to phrase...I don't want to irritate you but I want...Is there anyway...Is there someone we might be able to contact that might be able release you from your vow of secrecy? Is there somewhere we might be able to go that we might be able to get permission for you to talk?

EDE: Not that I know of.

KDR: If we got some orders from the Pentagon, would that be sufficient? If they came from the right place?

EDE: I just don't want to talk about it. Sorry about it.

KDR: All right, sir. I understand. I spent fifteen years in the Air Force myself as an Intelligence Officer so I understand completely where you're coming from, sir.

EDE: There was another Intelligence Officer but I can't remember his name. Freeze?

KDR: There was a Breece.

EDE: Breece. Have you talked to him?

KDR: We haven't been able to find him. Do you know where he might be?

EDE: No, I sure don't. Really, I sure don't. I haven't had contact with him for years. I'm not sure if I left there first or that he did.

KDR: Breece actually left out there in, I believe, August of 1947. We have a phone book, of course he's in the phone book too. We have a phone book from August of 1947 with your name in it as the Provost Marshal. Breece of course assigned to Jesse Marcel's office. You phone number was three six five, but the way...some of the records we have suggest that Captain Breece left in August or September of 1947. You were the Provost Marshal.

EDE: That's right.

KDR: The Provost Marshal would be in command of the military police out there?

EDE: Yes.

KDR: Was the MP company under your direct supervision?

EDE: That's right.

KDR: But you were not a member of that company?

EDE: If I remember, they were assigned to Squadron A for administration etc.

KDR: Well we've got a yearbook from the 509th Bomb Group which which had Captain Tripp in command of the MP Company.

EDE: Well, he worked for me.

KDR: He worked for you?

EDE: That's right.

KDR: That was just some of the logistics that I wanted to get straight in my mind. But there isn't really much that you can do to help me out then?

EDE: Not I'm sorry. I really am.

KDR: Have you considered writing memoir? We were just hoping that someday we could get at the whole story.

EDE: Well, I think you'd better start up at the top at the Pentagon...they could probably put you on the right track.

KDR: All right, sir. I don't want to keep you. I appreciate the little help that you could give me.

EDE: That's all right.

KDR: I hope you don't mind me bothering you. I just don't know where to go with this thing now. I don't want to ask you a question that's going to irritate you.

EDE: Oh, I'm not going to be irritated. I think if you start at the top you'll come out a lot better. Get in there and find somebody that has some information and you might be able to get what you're after.

KDR: Well , Colonel Briley was able to help us a little bit...as the Operations Officer. And we've talked to one of the counterintelligence agents who told us, in fact, that the Provost Marshal was on the crash site.

EDE: He doesn't know what he's talking about.

KDR: And that the MPs had the area cordoned off.

EDE: What else?

KDR: We've got quite a bit of information like that.

MPs had the area cordoned off on the morning of July 8, 1947. That the local police force was turned back frown it. That the MPs had the area, the roads blocked going in. That a number of people, soldiers were brought in to clean up the debris field. Stuff was loaded on trucks and taken into the Roswell Army Airfield and flown out on a number of different flights.

EDE: You should probably get that information to the intelligence people.

KDR: Do you know of any of the intelligence people who might have been out there?

EDE: I just know that intelligence people were stationed there.

KDR: If I think of anything that you might be able to answer would it be all right if I called you back?

EDE: That'd be all right.

KDR: Okay. Well, thank you very much sir.

EDE: You're welcome.

Proctor, Loretta, Brazel neighbor, Transcript of Interview April 20, 1989

KDR: Do you have a few minutes to talk right now?

LP: I have a few minutes to talk to you.

KDR: As you know we're looking into the incident there from 1947.

LP: Yes.

KDR: I understand that you know a little about it.

LP: Well, not much. I just...I didn't see it. All I can tell you is just hearsay and what was written in the book.

KDR: Did you or your husband possibly go out and take a look?

LP: No, he didn't. Back then, why gas, tires, time and everything was real short.

KDR: They he wasn't expecting to see an alien spacecraft or anything.

LP: Oh no. We just figured it was a weather balloon or an experiment or something.

KDR: Did you talk to Mac Brazel about it afterwards at all?

LP: Well, before he took it in, but after he took it to Roswell he wouldn't talk about it.

KDR: I understand this was forty years ago...you don't happened to know the exact chronology of the events do you?

LP: No, I don't really. I'm getting old myself and forgetful.

KDR: Do you remember anything he might have said before going to Roswell about it? Didn't he visit you at the house.

LP: Yes, he came up and wanted us to go down and see it. We told him that if he thought he had something he had something...you know, we'd heard there was a reward out for a UFO, he might, you know, take it and report it down there. I guess he did.

KDR: You'd heard there was a reward for UFOs at the time?

LP: Well, that was the tale at the time. People thought, well, you know.

KDR: There were actually newspaper stories that there was three thousand dollars for proof positive that you had a flying saucer.

LP: Yeah, something like that.

KDR: I've come across those stories several times. Did he describe what he'd found to you at all?

LP: Well, yes. And he did bring a little sliver of a wood looking stuff up but you couldn't burn it or you couldn't or anything. I guess it was just a little sliver of, or about the size of a pencil and about three or four inches long.

KDR: Do you remember what color it was?

LP: Well, I would say that it was kind of a brownish tan but you know that's been quite a long time. It looked, of course, there wasn't any plastic then but that was kind of what it looked like.

KDR: When he brought it up did you attempt to cut it or anything?

LP: No, we didn't. He did and he was telling us about

more about the other material that was so light weight and that was crinkly up and then would fold out. And, I can't remember if he brought a scrap of that or not. But he said there was some more stuff in there, like a tape that had some sort of figures on it and it wasn't any kind of writing that either or print or anything that we knew that was written on it.

KDR: Did he talk about finding something that might have been more intact than the pieces of it that he mentioned?

LP: He never did say what he had. But anyway, he went into Roswell and reported it and they flew him back out there to show then the location and they took him back to Roswell and kept him down there until they got it all cleaned up.

KDR: So once he went to Roswell there was a flight back over the ranch area then.

LP: I guess they came up in a truck or whatever they hauled it in. I don't know how many came up or anything.

KDR: You didn't see any military people?

LP: Oh no. It's maybe twenty miles down there.

KDR: Is you house in the same location as 1947?

LP: Oh yes. It's in the same place.

KDR: So if they'd come up on the Pine Lodge Road, you'd have never seen them.

LP: Oh no. It's forty miles from here to the Pine Lodge Road. From where that was found, I don't know, I imagine it was at least twenty miles.

KDR: Do you know if there was more than one found or was it all in one place?

LP: That was the only one I knew of.

KDR: Did you talk to Ralph Hieck? I guess you know him pretty

LP: No, not too well.

KDR: Did you kind of tell him where you thought it was?

LP: Well, from what I had heard from over there, I thought it was over close to what we call the twin mills, south or maybe southwest. I don't really know the exact area. It was right in that area somewhere. I was never to the place so I really can't tell anybody where it was because we didn't go over.

KDR: I bet you wish had now, don't you?

LP: Well, yes. But, you know, at that time, why, people were having a hard time even making a living. Their tires, their gas, everything, their time, kind of limited you. You didn't...

KDR: Do you remember anything Mac Brazel might have told you when he first came up?

LP: He just told us about finding this strange object or whatever. We told him...you know, he ought to report it.

KDR: Mac didn't have a phone at that time, did he?

LP: No.

KDR: Did you have a phone?

LP: No. We didn't get a phone until about three years ago. It was all horseback or a car.

KDR: Do you know where he might have gone to use a phone? Would he have had to go into Corona?

LP: He went to Roswell, I'm sure.

KDR: He didn't call anyone? He went to Roswell first?

LP: I think he probably just took some of it down and reported it and they brought him back out and took him back and kept checking until they got all of it. I sure that's the way it happened. They did keep him down there several days.

KDR: Do you know who all was at his ranch?

LP: There weren't very many there. Our seven year old son was with him when he found it but he can't remember where it was at and he can't remember what it looked like.

KDR: You son was with him?

LP: Yeah, he was staying down there with Mac. Mac was by himself at that time. He might have had one other hand but Bill was still living in Albuquerque when...and Paul was working on the ranch down in Texas.

KDR: Was Bessie with him?

LP: No, she wasn't at the ranch when this happened. Some of them kind of got their stories mixed up. No, she wasn't there.

KDR: So your son was there?

LP: They were on horseback when they found it. It was a good many years ago and a little ole seven year old kid won't remember much. He don't remember.

KDR: So all they found, basically, was bits and pieces of the thing spread out over a field?

LP: Well, it wasn't over a field. It was out in a pasture.

KDR: Has anyone ever talked to your son about this?

LP: Not...he don't say anything because he really can't remember. He was seven years old. You don't remember any details. It just didn't impress him.

KDR: Do you think he'd be willing to at least say hi to me?

LP: Well, he's not around now. He says that he's not going to talk to anyone about it because I don't remember anything about it. I don't want people thinking I'm trying to talk about it.

Mac brought him home and told us about it. He didn't go to Roswell or anything.

KDR: So he wouldn't be aware if the Air Force cordoned off the area or anything?

LP: No, it's something that happened way back there.

KDR: What do you think it was?

LP: I believe in UFOs. I've seen so many strange lights and things...I think that we're here there could be somebody out there. But if they are they're so much ahead of us that...you get to thinking about how far we've come in the last several years. I can remember the first radio I ever saw and I sure can remember the first television. It's possible that out there there is some other life like we're here.

KDR: So your basic involvement with this whole story is that Mac Brazed brought your son back and had a piece of this material with him.

LP: Just a little sliver of it. That's all he had with him.

KDR: Did you ever ask him about it after he got back from Roswell?

LP: He just said that it was a weather balloon. Whatever they told him down there. He wouldn't talk about it. He did say that if I ever find another I'm not going to report it. But he said it was a weather balloon. They'd convinced him it was or something.

KDR: Is Robert Porter your son?

LP: My brother.

KDR: He was on an airplane that went to Fort Worth, I understand.

LP: At that time they were training, I don't know if you even know what the silver plate division was...the ones that dropped the atomic bomb. They were training there in Roswell. He was with that bunch. And his crew was the ones that flew it out of Roswell whatever it was. He said they covered it up. They didn't know where they were going or what they were taking.

KDR: Could you give me his number in Great Falls.

LP: You haven't talked to him?

KDR: No, I've got a friend who's talked to him. Then I was going to ask you if you'd ask him if he wouldn't mind chatting with me about it. I understand that he was seven years old and it didn't make much of an impression...

LP: I don't think he'll know anything to tell you.

KDR: To due the investigation properly we should at

least contact him to let him tell us that he doesn't remember anything. He might remember something right off the wall that would help us out tremendously.

LP: My brother's phone number is xxx-xxx-xxxx.

KDR: Is there anything else that you can remember about this that might help us out?

LP: No, I know that the day after Mac went to Roswell it made all the news. And then it hushed up real quick. You just never heard any more about it.

KDR: I just feel there is something else that I should ask you but I don't know what it would be.

LP: Really, I think it's kind of a lost cause that far back. The ones that were there are gone.

KDR: Did you ever hear anything about bodies or anything like that?

LP: No. If Mac had found them I'm sure he would have said something about it.

KDR: How about railroad men around the area? There was a story that a bigger chunk of it was taken out by railroad.

LP: I don't think so. I never heard that.

KDR: Tommy Tyree. Was he working with Mac at the time?

LP: He went to work with him later. He wasn't working down there at that time.

KDR: Bill talked about finding a few finding a few scraps of the material and then talking about it in Corona. The next day someone came and took it from him. Had you seen, or do you know of any strangers in the area who might have been the one watching.

LP: No. I don't think there was.

KDR: You didn't see any military people or equipment?

LP: No, I didn't see anything like that.

KDR: Well, shoot, I just can't think of anything else.

LP: There's been too much water under the bridge.

KDR: Listen, if I think of anything more would it be okay if I called you back?

LP: Okay. That'd be fine.

Roberts, Jud (George), Reporter, KGFL Radio, Roswell, Transcript, January 19, 1990

KDR: My name's Kevin Randle, and I talked to Art McQuiddy just a few minutes ago. I was trying to get some information on this Roswell event that took place in July of 1947.

GFR: I didn't know too much about it.

KDR: Art said that you might be able to help me out a little bit.

GFR: All right.

KDR: He said that you worked at the radio station there?

GFR: Yes. Uh-huh.

KDR: With Walt Whitmore?

GFR: Well, W.E.

KDR: W.E.

GFR: Yes.

KDR: Senior?

GFR: Yes.

KDR: We understand that Walt has spirited Mac Brazel away from the military at some point and hid him out...

GFR: Hide him out overnight, that's all.

KDR: Were you involved in that at all?

GFR: Not really. I was running the station. I was the station manager.

KDR: And this was W.G...?

GFR: W.E. Whitmore.

KDR: No the station call letters?

GFR: KGFL. That was the original station. Did I meet you out to the airport once with Art when the film crew was coming in?

KDR: I was involved in the *Unsolved Mysteries* thing, so I was involved in that. You might have seen me on that. I didn't get out to the airport with that. Did you get a chance to talk to Mac Brazel at all?

GFR: No, not that I recall. He was kind...we were kind of hurrying on him to get him out of there. We wanted an exclusive on the thing of course, if we could.

KDR: Oh, of course.

GFR: So when we, when there were some questions about releasing it and so forth, why, we got a notice that if we released it, our license would be gone the second day, so we didn't do very much on it at that time. No, we just ducked him out so that we could talk to him ahead of time, don't you see? Because they were looking for him. Now, Walt Haut, as you know, was the PIO out there.

KDR: Talked to Walt a number of times.

GFR: Of course you have. He was a good guy out there, and we knew him for the time he was about a second lieutenant I guess. But I wish I could give you a whole lot more, but really I haven't...the matter, of course, has been discussed on several occasions. But all we did is that one other guy went out with Whit and they brought Brazel in and then they hid him out on East Second at Whit's house overnight for whatever reason, I don't know.

KDR: Do you know who the other fellow is who went

out with him?

GFR: Oh, I wouldn't have the slightest idea. We didn't ...admittedly we didn't have that big a crew at that time. I think that probably that...I'm trying to think of who we might have had at that time...I really don't know. It might have been just one of Whit's pals around the place, don't you know...around the town. I know that if it were somebody who worked there, I would have no idea because almost all of them I know have passed away that I know about, or even remembered about.

KDR: Do you remember Frank Joyce at all?

GFR: Oh sure. Sure. I don't know. It's possible that it might have been Frank. Frank was a guy who was an announcer and a newsman. He was a very busy guy... (chuckles)...if it was TDY time, we always needed to think about what might happen when somebody came back from England after a 96-day TDY of something. But he was a bachelor and he became a pretty active fellow. As a matter of fact, was a fine announcer. But kind of hard to predetermine when he might be there and when he might be there and when he might be gone. But he's still working out at KOB. My gosh, he's been there for a hundred years.

KDR: I've actually talked to him. I watched a couple of his ski and fishing reports.

GFR: Oh, sure. He was a fine announcer. At that particular time, anyone who could pronounce anything was kind of an oddity because that, as I remember it, I think that was a hundred, might have been a hundred and fifty, might have been a 250 watter. I don't think so. It was the first one that I'd ever been in that was that size. Might even have been a hundred watter at that particular time, which was the latter part of the summer in '46 when I came down here.

Put anyway, there was considerable talk and so forth,

but there wasn't any question that it didn't take very long before nobody could get within gunshot (wound) of that area out there. It was all tied off.

KDR: Did you attempt to get out there yourself?

GFR: Yeah, we went out to just off the perimeter.

KDR: Did you see the military on the perimeter there?

GFR: Sure.

KDR: Now this is the crash site?

GFR: Well, it was presumed to be. Well, it's where they found the stuff on his ranch.

KDR: But you went into...actually into the Corona area, to the ranch area where it was found.

GFR: Yeah, we went out there, but couldn't get in there. That was afterwards, and it was sealed off. Then, of course, there was lots of discussion and, oh gosh, the provost marshall out at Walker whose name now escapes me...he was transferred out of there in just a couple of weeks.

KDR: His name was Easley.

GFR: Is that right? Marcel or something.

KDR: No, Marcel was the intelligence officer.

GFR: Yeah, okay. He was transferred as you well know from your own notes. That was in a hurry. They moved him out right away. Walt took quite a little brunt on that thing. Pretty courageously as a matter of fact. They...our staff from Washington about our license.

KDR: You wouldn't remember who called you about that would you?

GFR: No, I wouldn't have any idea, but I imagine it was Clinton Anderson's office. He ran everything from there from the standpoint of the state.

KDR: Now that was Senator Anderson?

GFR: Oh sure. Clinton D. Anderson.

KDR: My partner, Don Schmitt and I are gong to be down there in the Roswell area next week. Could we stop by and say hello?

GFR: Well, of course, I'd love to see you.

KDR: Okay. Maybe I could go over some of the stuff with you in a little more. I'd like to talk to you about trying to go to the site and getting turned back by the military only because that confirms things we've heard from a number of other people. Did the military ever come to the station to go through the records and take back anything relating to the event?

GFR: No, not that I recall. The threat of the FCC was enough, don't you see?

KDR: You lose your license and you're all done.

GFR: Oh sure. Why don't you give me a ring when you're coming in?

KDR: Okay.

We finally talked about setting up a meeting during our trip down to Roswell.

STATEMENT OF HELEN CAHILL

(1) My name is Helen Cahill.

(2) My address is:

(3) During a visit from my parents (Mr. and Mrs. Dan Dwyer) in 1948, my father told me that something very important had happened but that he was not able to tell me what it was. He said that he was concerned about the safety of the family if he told. He mentioned that I was better off not knowing.

(4) During that same visit, my mother confirmed that something had happened and that my father wished he could tell me about it but he was afraid for the family. My mother said that my father was afraid that someone would come out to kill me if they thought he had told me anything.

(5) My sister, Frankie, told me about her experiences sometime in the early 1960s. Frankie told me about sitting around the table in 1947 and being threatened. My sister also mentioned seeing the material that "ran like water."

(6) I have not been paid or given anything of value to make this statement, which is the truth to the best of my recollection.

Helen L Cahill
(Signature)

11-22-93
(Date)

Signature witnessed by:

(Name)

STATE OF NEW MEXICO, COUNTY OF CURRY ss.
Subscribed and sworn to before me this 22nd day of November, 1993
Notary Public
My commission expires: 12-11-94

AFFIDAVIT

(1) My name is Thomas Jefferson DuBose.

(2) My address is:

(3) I retired from the U.S. Air Force in 1959 with the rank of Brigadier General.

(4) In July 1947, I was stationed at Fort Worth Army Air Field [later Carswell Air Force Base] in Fort Worth, Texas. I served as Chief of Staff to Major General Roger Ramey, Commander, Eighth Air Force. I had the rank of Colonel.

(5) In early July, I received a phone call from Maj. Gen. Clements McMullen, Deputy Commander, Strategic Air Command. He asked what we knew about the object which had been recovered outside Roswell, New Mexico, as reported by the press. I called Col. William Blanchard, Commander of the Roswell Army Air Field and directed him to send the material in a sealed container to me at Fort Worth. I so informed Maj. Gen. McMullen.

(6) After the plane from Roswell arrived with the material, I asked the Base Commander, Col. Al Clark, to take possession of the material and to personally transport it in a B-26 to Maj. Gen. McMullen in Washington, D.C. I notified Maj. Gen. McMullen, and he told me he would send the material by personal courier on his plane to Benjamin Chidlaw, Commanding General of the Air Materiel Command at Wright Field [later Wright Patterson AFB]. The entire operation was conducted under the strictest secrecy.

(7) The material shown in the photographs taken in Maj. Gen. Ramey's office was a weather balloon. The weather balloon explanation for the material was a cover story to divert the attention of the press.

(8) I have not been paid or given anything of value to make this statement, which is the truth to the best of my recollection.

T. J. DuBose

(Signature)

9/16/91

(Date)

Signature witnessed by:

Linda R. Split

(Name)

Notary Public
State of Florida
County of Orange

Notary Public, State of Florida
My Commission Expires Dec. 2, 1991
Bonded Thru Troy Fain - Insurance, Inc.

AFFIDAVIT OF BARBARA DUGGER

(1) My name is Barbara Dugger.

(2) My address is:

(3) I am employed by:

(4) My grandmother was Inez Wilcox, and my grandfather was George Wilcox, who was the Sheriff in Chaves County, New Mexico, in 1947. I lived with my grandmother while I was teaching at the New Mexico Military Institute. I was 24 years old at the time.

(5) One evening, while we were watching a TV program about space, my grandmother told me that in the 1940s, there was a spacecraft--a flying saucer--that crashed outside Roswell. She told me not to tell anybody, because when the event occurred, "the military police came to the jailhouse and told George and I that if we ever told anything about the incident, not only would we be killed, but our entire family would be killed." I said, "Did you believe them?" She said, "What do you think? They meant it, Barbara--they were not kidding." She didn't remember the names of those involved, however, she said it was Air Force personnel who threatened them. She never told anyone else in my family about the event, even my mother, Elizabeth Tulk.

(6) She said someone had come to Roswell and told him about this incident. My grandfather went out there to the site; it was in the evening. There was a big burned area, and he saw debris. He also saw four "space beings." One of the little men was alive. Their heads were large. They wore suits like silk.

(7) After he returned to his office, my grandfather got phone calls from all over the world--including England. MPs came to the jail. A lot of people came in and out of the jail at the time.

(8) She said the event shocked him. He never wanted to be sheriff again after that. Grandmother ran for sheriff and was defeated. She wrote an article about the event right after it happened to see if anyone else knew anything about it.

(9) My grandmother was a very loyal citizen of the United States, and she thought it was in the best interest of the country not to talk about the event. However, if she said it happened, it happened. Her state of mind was excellent at the time of this conversation. She was working in real estate. Grandfather had passed away by this time from hardening of the arteries. Grandmother passed away at age of 93.

(10) I have not been paid or given anything of value to make this statement, which is the truth to the best of my recollection.

Barbara Dugger
(Signature

Signature witnessed by:

Veronica Garcia

2-24-95
(Date)

AFFIDAVIT

(1) My name is Walter Haut.

(2) My address is:

(3) I am retired.

(4) In July 1947, I was stationed at the Roswell Army Air base, serving as the base Public Information Officer. At approximately 9:30 AM on July 8, I received a call from Col. William Blanchard, the base commander, who said he had in his possession a flying saucer or parts thereof. He said it came from a ranch northwest of Roswell, and that the base Intelligence Officer, Major Jesse Marcel, was going to fly the material to Fort Worth.

(5) Col. Blanchard told me to write a news release about the operation and to deliver it to both newspapers and the two radio stations in Roswell. He felt that he wanted the local media to have the first opportunity to have the story. I went first to KGFL, then to KSWS, then to the *Daily Record* and finally to the *Morning Dispatch*.

(6) The next day, I read in the newspaper that General Roger Ramey in Forth Worth had said the object was a weather balloon.

(7) I believe Col. Blanchard saw the material, because he sounded positive about what the material was. There is no chance that he would have mistaken it for a weather balloon. Neither is there any chance that Major Marcel would have been mistaken.

(8) In 1980, Jesse Marcel told me that the material photographed in Gen. Ramey's office was not the material he had recovered.

(9) I am convinced that the material recovered was some type of craft from outer space.

(10) I have not been paid nor given anything of value to make this statement, and it is the truth to the best of my recollection.

Walter G Haut
(Signature)

5-14-93
(Date)

Signature witnessed by:

Max Littell
(Name)

AFFIDAVIT

(1) My name is John Kromschroeder, DDS.

(2) My address is:

(3) I am retired from the field of dentistry.

(4) I met Oliver W. "Pappy" Henderson in 1962 or 1963. I learned that we shared an interest in metallurgy. We participated in several joint business ventures.

(5) In 1977, which was the 30th anniversary of Roswell event, Henderson told me about the Roswell incident. He said he transported wreckage and alien bodies to Wright Field in Dayton, Ohio. He described the wreckage as "spacecraft garbage." He said "the passengers suffered their death." He described the beings as small.

(6) Approximately one year later, Henderson produced a piece of metal taken from the craft. I gave it a good thorough looking at and decided that it was an alloy that we are not familiar with. It was a gray lustrous metal resembling aluminum, but lighter in weight and much stiffer.

(7) I have not been paid or given anything of value to make this statement, which is the truth to the best of my recollection.

Dr. John G. Kromschroeder
(Signature)

1 May, 1991
(Date)

Signature witnessed by:

John ...
(Name) Lcdr US Navy (Ret)

Claude J. Gabbar

AFFIDAVIT

TO WHOM IT MAY CONCERN:

On a night during July, 1947, I, James Ragsdale, was in the company of a woman in an area approximately forty (40) miles northwest of Roswell, New Mexico, during a severe lightning storm. I and my companion observed a bright flash and what appeared to be a bright light source moving toward the southeast. Later, at sunrise, driving in that direction, I and my companion came upon a ravine near a bluff that was covered with pieces of unusual wreckage, remains of a damaged craft and a number of smaller bodied beings outside the craft. While observing the scene, I and my companion watched as a military convoy arrived and secured the scene. As a result of the convoy's appearance we quickly fled the area.

I hereby swear the aforementioned account is accurate and true to the best of my knowledge and recollection.

James Ragsdale
James Ragsdale

STATE OF NEW MEXICO)
)ss
County of Chaves)

The foregoing instrument was acknowledged before me this 27TH day of JANUARY, 1993, by JAMES RAGSDALE.

My Commission expires:
11-7-96

Notary Public

AFFIDAVIT OF GEORGE "JUD" ROBERTS

(1) My name is George "Jud" Roberts.

(2) My address is:

(3) I am (X) retired ( ) employed as: ______________________.

(4) In July 1947, I was a minority stockholder and manager of KGFL Radio in Roswell, New Mexico. We did an interview with W.W. "Mac" Brazel, the rancher who found some debris on his property. We hid him out at the home of the station owner, W.E. Whitmore, Sr., and recorded the interview on a wire recorder.

(5) The next morning, I got a call from someone in Washington, D.C. It may have been someone in the office of Clinton Anderson or Dennis Chavez. This person said, "We understand that you have some information, and we want to assure you that if you release it, it's very possible that your station's license will be in jeopardy, so we suggest that you not do it." The person indicated that we might lose our license in as quickly as three days. I made the decision not to release the story.

(6) I made an attempt to go out to the crash site to see it for myself, but I was turned back by a military person who said we were in a restricted area.

(7) At that time, there was quite a clamp on any discussion concerning this event. We just decided for Walter Haut's sake that we should sit tight and not say anything, even though in our own minds, we had some question about the validity of the weather balloon explanation. Weather balloons were launched about a block from our station every day. We didn't accept the official explanation, but we had no evidence to the contrary.

(8) I have not been paid or given anything of value to make this statement, which is the truth to the best of my recollection.

George J. "Jud" Roberts
(Signature)

12/30/91
(Date)

Signature witnessed by:
SIGNATURE GUARANTEED
SUNWEST BANK OF ROSWELL, N.M.
(Name) ROSWELL, NEW MEXICO
BY Nancy Montgomery
Assistant Cashier

STATEMENT OF FRANKIE ROWE

(1) My name is Frankie Rowe.

(2) My address is:

(3) In July 1947, my father was a fire fighter with the Roswell, New Mexico Fire Department. He returned one night, telling the family that he had been on a fire run to the north of Roswell. There he encountered the wreck of some kind of craft and the bodies of the alien flight crew.

(4) In early July 1947, I was in the fire house waiting for my father to take me home. A State Trooper arrived and displayed a piece of metallic debris that he said he'd picked up on the crash site. It was a dull gray and about the thickness of aluminum foil. When wadded into ball, it would unfold itself. The fire fighters were unable to cut it or burn it.

(5) A few days later, several military personnel visited the house, telling my younger brothers and sisters to wait outside. My mother and I were told to sit at the dining room table where I was questioned about the piece of metal I had seen. I was told that if I ever talked about it, I could be taken out into the desert never to return, or that my mother and father would be taken to "Orchard Park", a former POW camp.

(6) I have not been paid or given anything of value to make this statement, which is the truth to the best of my recollection.

Frankie M. Rowe
(Signature)

11-22-93
(Date)

Signature witnessed by:

(Name)

STATE OF NEW MEXICO, COUNTY OF CURRY ss.
Subscribed and sworn to before me this 22nd day
of November, 1993
Keitha Watkins
Notary Public
My commission expires:
12-11-94

AFFIDAVIT

(1) My name is Robert E. Smith.

(2) My address is:

(3) I am (X) retired ( ) employed by______________________________.

(4) In July 1947, I was stationed at the Roswell Army Air Field as a member of the 1st Air Transport Unit. I worked in the cargo outfit with C-54s. My involvement in the Roswell incident was to help load crates of debris on to the aircraft. We all became aware of the event when we went to the hangar on CENTERS the east side of the ramp. Our people had to re-measure the ~~aircraft on the inside~~ to accommodate the ~~crates~~ they were making for this material. All I AIRCRAFT saw was a little piece of material. The piece of debris I saw was two-to-three inches square. It was jagged. When you crumpled it up, it then laid back out; and when it did, it kind of crackled, making a sound like cellophane, and it crackled when it was let out. There were no creases. One of our people put it in his pocket.

(5) The largest piece was roughly 20 feet long; four-to-five feet high, four-to-five feet wide. The rest were two-to-three feet long, two feet square or smaller. The sergeant who had the piece of material said that was the material in the crates. There were words stenciled on the crates, but I don't remember what they were; however, the word "section" appeared on most of the crates. The entire loading took at least six, perhaps eight hours. Lunch was brought to us, which was unusual. The crates were brought to us on flatbed dollies, which also was unusual.

(6) A lot of people began coming in all of a sudden because of the official investigation. Somebody said it was a plane crash; but we heard from a man in Roswell that it was not a plane crash but it was something else, a strange object. Officially, we were told it was a crashed plane, but crashed planes usually were taken to the salvage yard, not flown out. I don't think it was an experimental plane, because not too many people in that area were experimenting with planes--the didn't have the money to.

(7) We were taken to the hangar to load crates. There was a lot of farm dirt on the hangar floor. We loaded it on flatbeds and dollies; each crate had to be checked as to width and height. We had to know which crates went on to which plane. We loaded crates on to three or four C-54s. It took the better part of the day to load the planes. One crate took up the entire plane; it wasn't that heavy, but it was a large volume.

(8) This would have involved [Oliver W.] "Pappy" Henderson's crew. I remember seeing Tech Sgt. Harbell Ellzey and Sgt. T/Sgt. Edward Bretherton and S/Sgt. William Fortner; Elszey was on "Pappy's" crew.

(9) We weren't supposed to know the destination, but we were told they were headed north. Wright Field at that time was closed down for modernization; therefore, I would deduce that the next safest place was Los Alamos, the most secret base available and still under the Manhattan Project. There were armed guards present during the loading of the planes, which was unusual. There was

no way to get to the ramp except through armed guards. There were MPs on the outer skirts, and our personnel were between them and the planes.

(10) There were a lot of people in plainclothes all over the place; they were "inspectors," but they were strangers on the base. When challenged, they replied that they were here on project so-and-so and flashed a card, which was different than a military ID card.

(11) There was another indication that something serious was going on: several nights before this, when we were coming back to Roswell, a convoy of trucks covered with canvas passed us. The truck convoy had red lights and sirens. When they got to the gate, they headed over to this hangar on the east end, which was rather unusual.

(12) I have a distant cousin who was in the Secret Service named Raymond deVinney. In the early 1970s, at a family reunion, he told me that he was at Roswell at this time, more or less as a representative of President Truman. He saw me and recognized me, but he didn't speak. He said the material most likely was taken to Los Alamos. He said there were several people with him at the time, but he didn't mention any names. He passed away in 1975.

(13) A lot of the people involved in the event believe that they should go to their deathbeds without telling anything about it. We were told: "This is a hot shipment; keep quiet about it." This wasn't unusual for us--there were a lot of times we were told that.

(14) I'm convinced that what we loaded was a UFO that got into mechanical problems. Even with the most intelligent people, things go wrong.

(15) I have not been paid or given anything of value to make this statement, which is the truth to the best of my recollection.

Robert Earl Smith
(Signature)

10/10/91
(Date)

Signature witnessed by:

Pagon M Short
(Name)

PAGON M. SHORT
Notary Public
STATE OF TEXAS
My Comm. Exp. 05/31/93

AFFIDAVIT
William M. Woody

(1) My name is William M. Woody.

(2) My address is

(3) I am employed as:__________________________. ( ) I am retired.

(4) In 1947 I was 12 years old and living with my family on our farm, located south of Roswell, New Mexico, and east of what was then Roswell Army Air Field. I still live on that farm.

w.m.w. 14

w.m.w 3 south of

(5) One hot night during the summer of 1947, probably in early July, my father and I were outside on the farm. It was well after sundown and quite dark. Suddenly, the sky lit up. When we looked up to see where the light was coming from, we saw a large, very bright object in the southwestern sky, moving rapidly northward.

(6) The object had the bright white intensity of a blow torch, and had a long, flame-like tail, with colors like a blow-torch flame fading down into a pale red. Most of the tail was this pale red color. The tail was very long, equal to about 10 diameters of a full moon.

(7) We watched the object travel all the way across the sky until it disappeared below the northern horizon. It was moving fast, but not as fast as a meteor, and we had it in view for what seemed like 20 to 30 seconds. Its brightness and colors did not change during the whole time, and it definitely went out of sight below the horizon, rather than winking out like a meteor does. My father thought it was a big meteorite and was convinced it had fallen to earth about 40 miles north of Roswell, probably just southwest of the intersection of U.S. Highway 285 and the Corona road (State Highway 247).

(8) My father knew the territory, all its roads, and many of the people very well, so two or three days later (definitely not the next day), he decided to look for the object. He took me with him in our old flatbed truck. We headed north through Roswell on U.S. 285. About 19 miles north of town, where the highway crosses the Macho Draw, we saw at least one uniformed soldier stationed beside the road. As we drove along, we saw more sentries and Army vehicles. They were stationed at all places--ranch roads, crossroads, etc.--where there was access to leave the highway and drive east or west, and they were armed, some with rifles, others with sidearms. I do not remember seeing any military activity on the ranchland beyond the highway right of way.

(9) We stopped at one sentry post, and my father asked a soldier what was going on. The soldier, who's attitude was very nice, just said his orders were not to let anyone leave 285 and go into the countryside.

w.m.w 9-28-93

(10) As we drove north, we saw that the Corona road (State 247), which runs west from Highway 285, was blocked by soldiers. We went on as far as Ramon, about nine miles north of the 247 intersection. There were sentries there, too. At Ramon we turned around and headed south and home.

(11) I remember my father saying he thought the Army was looking for something it had tracked on its way down. He may have gotten this from the soldier he spoke with during our drive up 285, but I am not sure.

(12) I also recall that two neighbors, both now dead, stopped by and told my father they had seen the same object we had seen. One said others in his family had seen it, too. There were also many rumors about flying saucers that summer, and I recall the weather balloon story, explaining away the report of a flying saucer crash near Corona. This seemed reasonable to us at the time.

(13) I have not been paid or given or promised anything of value to make this statement, which is the truth to the best of my recollection.

William M Woody
William M. Woody | 9-28-93
(Signature and Printed Name) | (Date)

Signature witnessed by:

Tracy L. Callaway
Tracy L. Callaway | 9.28.93
(Signature and Printed Name) | (Date)

Expires April 20, 1997

Winds Aloft and Project Mogul: Late Breaking Facts

When both the Air Force and Karl Pflock issued their reports claiming that Project Mogul was responsible for the debris found by Mac Brazel, they had no proof for it. No documentation was presented. In fact, the two flights they claimed, either No. 4 on June 4, 1947 or No. 9 on July 3, seemed to have no documentation at all. The Air Force and Pflock suspected flights had been made, but the proof was nonexistent.

As mentioned earlier, Dr. Albert Crary's diary, kept during the Project Mogul experiments, offered the documentation that both flights had been made. Since nothing of scientific value was learned by either flight, they had been left out of the reports.

We now know something about each of those flights and that allows us to find other documentation that is relevant. We know, for example, Flight No. 9 was launched at 7:30 PM on the evening of July 3. We know that the balloon launched before it, Flight No. 8, traveled to the northwest and fell into the Tularosa Valley. We know that the balloon launched after it, Flight No. 10, traveled to the northwest, was seen over Albuquerque, and last seen near Pueblo, Colorado. Given that data, we know that neither can account for the debris found by Brazel.

We can then speculate that Flight No. 9 or the culprit named by Pflock, traveled to the northwest. No compelling evidence has been presented to counter this belief. It is a reasonable extrapolation based on the evidence in hand. However, we can take it all a step farther.

The National Climatic Data Center in Asheville, NC has microfilmed copies of the winds aloft charts for 1947. While these charts cannot prove that what fell on the Brazel ranch was a Project Mogul balloon, they can exclude it. If the winds were blowing in the wrong direction, then it is clear that the balloons would have traveled away from the ranch. If, however, they were blowing in the right direction, the winds aloft can only show it was possible for a Mogul balloon to have fallen on the ranch, not that it did.

These data are not as complete as I would have liked them. Although the charts range from the surface to 20,000 feet, the winds at various reporting stations are often blank which means, simply, no data were available.

Four stations are of relevance to us. These are the stations at Tucson, Arizona; El Paso, Texas and Albuquerque and Roswell, New Mexico. No winds data are available from Alamogordo, the launching site of the Mogul balloons.

The relevant charts are those made at 8:30 PM, MST on July 3 and at 2:30 AM on July 4. The only data for the 20,000 foot level on July 3 (8:30 PM) is from Albuquerque showing the wind blowing to the west at 15 knots. At 16,000 feet the wind was blowing at Albuquerque to the northwest at 15 knots.

At 2:30 the following morning, seven hours after the launch, the winds at Roswell at 20,000 feet are blowing to the northwest at 20 knots. At 16,000 feet, the wind at Roswell is blowing to the west at 15 knots, and the wind at

Albuquerque is blowing to the northeast at 25 knots. Of course, if the balloon had reached Albuquerque, the wind blowing in that direction would push it farther to the north, away from the Brazel ranch.

At 10,000 feet, the winds are literally all over the chart. The El Paso winds are to the north at 20 knots, the winds at Roswell are to the northeast at 25 knots and the winds at Albuquerque are to the southeast at 15 knots. That last is interesting because it could be suggested that the balloon, reaching Albuquerque could be blown back toward the Brazel ranch.

At 8000 feet, the winds from El Paso are to the northeast at 20 knots; at Roswell to the northeast at 35 knots and at Albuquerque to southeast at 20 knots. But, at 8,000 feet, there is another factor to be added and that is the terrain. The mountains between Alamogordo and Roswell are more than 8000 feet high. The pass on the highway at Apache Junction is 7700 feet. If the balloon was at 8000 feet or lower, it would have hit the mountains.

At 5000 feet, the winds in Roswell are blowing north at 35 knots, and at El Paso are blowing to the northeast at 15 knots. The surface winds at Albuquerque are blowing to the east at 10, to the northwest in Roswell are 20 and in El Paso to the northeast at 15.

Between Albuquerque and the Brazel ranch is the northern end of the San Andres Mountains with peaks above 9000 feet. If the balloon stayed aloft long enough to reach Albuquerque, the winds there would have pushed it back, into the mountains. It would not have drifted to the Brazel ranch.

Terrain and the winds seem to effectively rule out Flight No. 9. When this data is added to the lack of documentation, and that is coupled to the statement of Dr. C.B. Moore, that he doesn't believe it was a Mogul balloon (meaning polyethylene), the conclusion is obvious. Flight

No. 9 did not drop on the Brazel ranch.

The data for Flight No. 4 isn't quite as persuasive. The documentation supplies no direct time for the launch, though it seems to have been made in the afternoon. Dr. Crary's diary said there was no balloon flight because of clouds, but that a flight with a sonobuoy was made. The winds at the significant reporting stations all suggest a balloon would have traveled to the east, rather than the northeast. Flight No. 5, which followed early on June 5 drifted to the east northeast and was recovered twenty-five miles east of Roswell.

The winds aloft data, however, tend to eliminate the Mogul balloons. Couple that to eyewitness testimony, the lack of documentation supporting any other theory, and the conclusions become evident. The Project Mogul balloons were not responsible for the debris found by Mac Brazel and therefore, do nothing to explain the events.